Rarely have I sensed, as I did with Born Free, *that a book had been 'lived out' in practice long before it was 'written out' on paper. It is clearly the case that contemporary culture is craving silence, solitude and centredness. And here we have an invitation – indeed an initiation – into a life that is both inspiring and practical, spiritual and human, and beautiful in every way.*

PETE GREIG
Founder, 24-7 Prayer International and Senior Pastor, Emmaus Rd Church

Born Free *touched my soul. Experience, so candidly described, opens a window into what is a common experience for many of us. It is the conflict between our heart's desire to know God in a deeper way and the lived reality of the relentless activity and hurriedness that militates against that. If we long for change, this book is a great place to start.*

ROB PARSONS OBE
Chairman and Founder, Care for the Family

In a society that adores talent from the stage, Katharine Hill is an emerging sage. And the church desperately needs her voice. She is sharp and sane and if you want to know what it means to be 'born free', this is the book for you.

DANIEL GROTHE
Associate Senior Pastor, New Life Church, Colorado Springs and Author of *The Power of Place*

Covid made us all stop! The lessons Katharine Hill learned are ones I too glimpsed but foolishly did not pause to ponder. I thank God she did, because there are so many insights about our souls, our Sundays, our phones, our drivenness and our rhythms of life, which we neglect at our peril. I also found this such an engaging, well-illustrated book, that I feel I could give it to any of my friends, regardless of their beliefs. It's a real tool for evangelism as well, as everyone reflects on their Covid journey.

RICO TICE
Senior Minister for Evangelism, All Souls Langham Place, London and Founder, Christianity Explored Ministries

When I read that Katharine Hill wrote this book for people like her, and she listed the struggles faced by Christians wanting to make a difference in the world while battling the relentless demands of a busy life, I found myself ticking almost every box. I've spent much of my life relying on performance to prove my worth. By the time I got to the end of the book, I felt lighter. I'd been challenged, encouraged and supported, with practical ideas to help me find space to experience the presence of God while living out my calling to minister in my family, business, community and church.

Through her wonderful use of relatable personal stories and preparedness to show her own vulnerability, Katharine manages to teach valuable lessons about how to order our priorities as Christians in today's world, and to provide very practical ideas about how to stick to them.

Though eminently readable, this isn't a book to be rushed through but to savour, to absorb a chapter at a time, to reflect on the questions at the end of each, to allow God to speak to you and 'cooperate with the Holy Spirit as he turns us more into the image of Christ.'

JOËLLE WARREN MBE
Founder and EOT Chair, Warren Partners

Longing to enjoy God deeply in everything? Katharine shares her hard-won wisdom to help busy people do just that.

Many will identify with Katharine's longing to love God more and the challenges of doing so in our busy, distracting world. So her hard-won wisdom shared with vulnerability and humility are a wonderful gift to those who seek to make space for the transforming work of God in the everyday.

With winsomeness and authenticity, Katharine shares wisdom that will help us all encounter God more deeply, even in today's busy, distracting world.

TRACY COTTERELL
Charity Trustee and Senior Mission Associate, London Institute for Contemporary Christianity (LICC)

I loved reading Born Free. *Katharine understands the issues around wellbeing and the dynamics of modern family and work pressures, and invites each of us to consider how we might live more deliberately, simply and freely. Packed with ancient wisdom and modern insight, this book suggests we can indeed flourish in the midst of our demanding lives. Highly recommended!*

CATHY MADAVAN

Speaker, writer, broadcaster and author of *Why Less Means More*

Katharine Hill's newest book combines a delicious concoction of biblical wisdom, targeted research and eminently practical advice from a woman of warmth and grace. Sit down to this feast, that – if you let it – will change the way you do the rest of your life. You'll push away from the table empowered to answer the call to 'be still, know God, and flourish in a hectic world'*!*

PHIL AND DIANE COMER

Founders, Intentional Parents International and Authors of *Raising Passionate Jesus Followers: The power of intentional parenting*

Katharine Hill takes us on a journey of a lifetime, to learn to live as one truly 'born free'. *Taking a little time to reflect on the very thought-provoking questions at the close of each chapter will make this deceptively easy read even more rewarding. Here is profound yet practical advice on the call to be still, know God and flourish in this hectic world.*

HANNELI RUPERT-KOEGELENBERG

Harmonie NPC, Franschhoek, South Africa

In Born Free, *Katharine tells her own story and it is both gripping and highly relevant to each one of us in the modern age. With her sharp mind and compelling style, Katharine uses lessons from the story of Elsa the lioness to describe what it means to live 'freely and lightly from a place of attentive stillness'. You will love this book!*

NICKY AND SILA LEE

Founders of The Marriage Course and authors of *The Marriage Book and The Parenting Book*

BORN
FREE

BORN
FREE

A CALL TO BE STILL, KNOW GOD
AND FLOURISH IN A HECTIC WORLD

KATHARINE HILL

FOREWORD BY JILL WEBER

Published in 2023 by

Muddy Pearl, Edinburgh, Scotland.

www.muddypearl.com

books@muddypearl.com

© Katharine Hill 2023

British Library Cataloguing in Publication Data

A catalogue record for this book is available from the British Library

HB ISBN 978-1-914553-18-9
PB ISBN 978-1-914553-13-4

Typeset in Minion by Revo Creative Ltd, Lancaster

Printed in Great Britain by Bell & Bain Ltd, Glasgow

To Kerry, who asks brilliant questions.

I think, if I had understood then, as I do now, how this great King really dwells within this little palace of my soul, I should not have left him alone so often. [1]

TERESA OF AVILA, *THE WAY OF PERFECTION*

CONTENTS

ACKNOWLEDGMENTS

The message in this book has been growing in my heart for years, but would never have seen the light of day without the encouragement, wisdom, challenge and example of so many people.

Thank you to Kerry McLeish whose question prompted this stage of my journey, and continues to encourage me on the way.

Thank you to Care for the Family's former Senior Editor, Sheron Rice, who agreed to give of her time, wisdom and incredible editing skills to help craft the book and added such value. A big thank you also to her successor Sarah Rowlands for her time and expertise.

I am very grateful to all those who read and commented on the manuscript, particularly Rob Parsons, Tracy Cotterell, Rich Wilson and Samantha Callan – it's a better book because of you – and special thanks to Jill Weber for writing the Foreword.

A huge thank you to the wonderful team at Care for the Family, and in particular to my PA Jody Jones. And once again to Stephanie Heald at Muddy Pearl – it is great working with you. Thank you for your expertise, care and attention to detail, encouragement and friendship.

I am especially grateful for those who shared their experiences with me. I have changed some details so that you remain anonymous, but your stories make all the difference.

John Mark Comer – I'm grateful we connected – your teaching was a kickstart on this journey. And although we have never met, Ruth Haley Barton has brought wisdom from afar. I am grateful to you both and also to others who are ahead of me on this road.

The proverb says 'iron sharpens iron', and so thank you to all those we have done life with over the years, in particular Annie and Silas, Jo, Jane and Ginny, the family from Christ Church Clifton, our small community, Nick and Lucy, Crossnet Bristol and the

OMS tribe on the first watch. You have all challenged, encouraged and enriched my life in ways you may never know.

And then to my own pride – Richard, George, Ellie, Eva and Arabella, Charlotte, Will, Ezra and Tabitha, Ed, Catriona, Finn and Henry – thank you! I couldn't ask for a more loyal or loving family, and our lives together are the context for many of the lessons in this book.

And finally to Elsa, the lioness whose story inspired this book in the first place … thank you.

FOREWORD

I'm a modern-day monastic, living on the Waverley Abbey Estate and working with the team here to renew this ancient monastery. I teach, work, and write, but my life is shaped by daily rhythms of prayer and extended times in God's presence. People often ask me, 'how much do you pray?' I hate giving an answer because I'm aware that as someone whose vocation is primarily prayer, I'm an oddity.

Most of us have got kids to drive to school, work commutes to make, gardens to tend, laundry to do, reports to write, bills to pay. Life can sometimes feel like we're strapped to a roller coaster, that it's going awfully fast, is occasionally hair-raising, and we can't get off the ride till the end. Or we're scurrying around, head down, powering through our to-do list, and carrying a vague sense of guilt or an undercurrent of worry. We are hungry for more of God than we are experiencing right now, but unsure how to carve out the necessary time and space to come and sit at His table and be fed in His presence.

How do ordinary people in their everyday lives experience the extraordinary grace and nearness of God from day to day? This is the question we ask ourselves as we look around for a teacher who shares our struggles.

Enter Katharine Hill. She is a dynamo. Energetic, confident, sharp. Warm, humble, and accessible.

This book is practical, accessible, well researched and thought through. It is a handbook of her hard-won wisdom. In it, Katharine unpacks not only the Scriptures and this cultural moment but also her own life experience. With vulnerability, transparency, and generosity, Katharine shares with us her own exploration of her internal resistance to a deepening life in God and the barriers she encountered along the way. Then she offers us her own personal toolkit to build a sustainable life that is deeply connected to the God who desires to walk with us and nourish us daily.

Katharine extends to us an invitation to spiritual transformation, which author Ruth Haley Barton describes as the process by which Christ is formed in us for our abundance, for the glory of God, and for the sake of others.[2] We can't transform ourselves, but we can, as it were, 'put ourselves in the path of oncoming grace', make space in our lives and hearts and open ourselves to God so that God can come and do the things in and through us that are beyond our natural inclinations and capacities.

They say that people teach what they know, but they only reproduce who they are. Orange trees may talk philosophy, but they will only bear oranges. The fruit of Katharine's journey is evident in her own character, her life and work as she champions and cheers on families across the UK and beyond.

'You can do this!' Katharine says, 'and here is how. How do I know? Because I've done it myself.'

Jill Weber

2 Ruth Haley Barton. Course Notes. The Transforming Community, 2011.

PREFACE

I wrote this book for people like me. People who want to experience more of the love of God, to love others more, to grow in their discipleship, experience life in the Spirit and make a difference in the world, but who struggle with the relentless demands of a busy life. People whose everyday reality includes the merry-go-round of battling the inbox, meeting project deadlines, changing nappies and surviving sleepless nights, refereeing toddler tantrums or riding the rollercoaster of the teenage years, handling difficult complaints, demanding patients or unreasonable supervisors, caring for ageing parents, running businesses, dealing with team conflict, leading churches, navigating traffic hold ups, delayed appointments and checkout queues. People worn down by financial worries, long working hours, health concerns, parenting angst, unwelcome singleness, infertility, a difficult boss, pressures in marriage or challenging relationships. People who every so often dream of stepping off the treadmill and retreating to a monastery, but who know that the season of life they are in and the responsibilities they carry make that course of action impossible.

As I've wrestled with this issue over the years, a troubling question has filled my mind. I've found myself wondering if growing deeper in our love for Jesus and engaging with the demands of everyday work and life are, in fact, mutually exclusive. Is making space to meet with God in a way that allows the possibility of transformational change simply naïve idealism? Or, at best, lofty rhetoric for the privileged few? Is that way of living just a pipe dream, attainable by the handful of people who can actually press the pause button and dial out of the commitments and pressures of normal life? In fact, is it remotely feasible in our always-on existence to live at anything like a sustainable pace, while growing in our love for God and for others?

In grappling with these questions, something gnawed at me deep inside, suggesting that this way of living *had* to be possible. So I began to ask what it might look like to live from a place of stillness, to 'keep company with Jesus' in the context of our lives as stay-at-home parents, business executives, artists, builders, civil servants, plumbers, computer technicians, lawyers, baristas, farmers, charity entrepreneurs, NHS workers, carers, pastors, students, teachers, during times of unemployment, or in the season of retirement … you fill in the blank.

Can we experience the freedom of a transforming relationship with God not in the leafy, shaded cloisters of a convent or the confines of a monastic cell, but right in the messiness and humdrum busyness of our 'sleeping, eating, going-to-work, and walking-around' everyday life (Romans 12:1, MSG)? Is there a way of living that not only benefits us but also has an impact on those around us and the communities we live in?

I am on the exciting journey of discovering glimpses of living in this way, and I hope this book will encourage you to do the same.

I have divided the book into two sections. Part One holds a magnifying glass to the roots of distraction and busyness in our lives that, if left unchecked, can either leave God out of the equation or at best relegate his presence to the sidelines.

Part Two invites us to a different way of living, encouraging us to learn how, right in the busyness of life, we can learn to live freely. And to stimulate our thinking, I have included a couple of questions at the end of each chapter to give readers an opportunity for personal reflection and response.

PART ONE

GO TO THE ANT ...

CHAPTER 1

A SIMPLE QUESTION

> On two occasions I watched her walk unconcernedly through
> a broad stream of black soldier ants, scattering their organized
> columns in all directions with her large paws.[3]

It seemed a stupid question – the kind that pops up with annoying
regularity on my social media feed and makes me hit the delete
button immediately. But on this occasion, I had a problem. It hadn't
come via social media; it was being asked by a wise and godly friend;
someone I'd built a relationship with over a number of years and
respected; someone who was not only wise but had the gift of asking
brilliant questions. So, however trivial it seemed, I felt I should at
least give it the time of day.

'If you were an animal, what animal would you be?'

As a matter of courtesy, I gave the question a few minutes' thought.
I found the answer came quite easily: I was an ant.

My husband Richard and I had recently taken our grandchildren
to the zoo and had spent a happy hour in Bug World. Little eyes
had marvelled at the range of mini beasts and creepy-crawlies on
display: locusts, spiders, beetles, and a platoon of leaf-cutter ants.
It was mesmerizing to watch the ants hard at work, marching in an
impressive, choreographed routine, some carrying leaves weighing
up to fifty times their body weight! And now, as I reflected on
the question, I realized that in many ways I behaved like these
impressive little creatures. I tended to be busy, reliable, productive
and focused, with the capacity to carry a heavy load. In the context

1 (Dedication page) St Teresa of Avila, *The Way of Perfection*, translated and edited by E. Allison Peers (Dead Authors Society, 2018), p170.
3 Joy Adamson, *Born Free* (Pantheon Books, 1960), p105.

of work, family, church – in fact, in every sphere of life – I was the kind of reliable, busy, high-capacity person that others came to when they not only wanted something done, but done well. People would often ask me, 'How do you fit it all in?'

I remembered that the writer of Proverbs commended the ant for her industry and hard work: 'Go to the ant, you sluggard; consider its ways and be wise!' (Proverbs 6:6), and in that moment, I rather liked the thought of being an ant. Repenting of my cynicism, I decided the question was a good one after all.

But then came a follow-up question that caught me unawares: 'If you could be any animal, what animal would you *like* to be?'

It is sobering when a simple question reveals an uncomfortable truth about our character and lifestyle. When I thought about my way of life – my place in the army of ants inexorably marching forward in formation – I was struck by the thought that perhaps it has a shadow side. While it felt good to have the reputation that I was someone who got lots done, being an ant seemed to offer a shallow and even prescriptive existence.

Ant behaviour is great if you are an ant. But I am not an ant. I am a woman with responsibilities and opportunities, hopes and dreams. I had a growing sense that something was lacking, somehow, I was missing out. Although I focused on the things I thought mattered, and my days were action-packed and full, my way of life felt small and one-dimensional. There was little margin. Little time for delight in unexpected pleasures, for time to linger, to listen, to reflect, to be still … Little time to grasp the 'extravagant dimensions' of the love of God (Ephesians 3:14–19, MSG).

I realized I didn't want to be an ant anymore.

I took a moment to consider the options. My musings took me to a wonderful trip I'd made to South Africa a few years before. My colleagues and I had been touring the country, speaking about parenting, and at the end of the trip our generous hosts arranged for us to go on a short safari. I can still picture the breathtaking beauty of the African landscape on the early morning and evening game drives, remember the smell of the rain on the dusty ground, hear the soundtrack of the crickets and cicadas, and feel the wonder of watching birds and animals roaming in their natural habitat – something I'd previously seen only in David Attenborough documentaries. One memory stands out in particular.

It was evening, with the sun beginning to set and casting long shadows across the ground, when the driver stopped our Jeep and pulled out his binoculars. Looking in the direction he was pointing us to, we saw a herd of zebra grazing in the golden light, the long grass swaying in the gentle breeze, catching the last rays of the sun. It was a magical scene. But our guide had seen something we missed: a lioness, lying motionless in the grass, her attention fixed on the zebra who were totally unaware of her presence. Holding our breath, we watched her inch forward towards her prey, and then settle down again. Occasionally, the zebra would look up and sniff the wind, but then continue to graze, oblivious to the danger. We waited in silence as the minutes ticked by, but the lioness didn't move. She was on a mission, peaceful, still and utterly focused. And she had all the time in the world.

We waited for the best part of an hour until, reluctantly, we had to continue on our way. Of course, we had a timetable to keep to, but the truth is that I could have watched that lioness all night. She was majestic, strong, confident and secure, hiding in plain sight and waiting for exactly the right moment to channel her powerful energy. The following day we saw her again, this time sitting underneath a tree, her forelegs stretched out in front of her, the toned muscles visible beneath her tawny coat. Surrounded by her cubs, she was peaceful and calm, confident in who she was as she scanned the horizon for movement. She was resting and yet fully alert, attentive to the moment, ready to jump up and go the distance at a second's notice. Attentive. And yet completely still. Attentive stillness.

And in that moment, I knew the answer: *I wanted to be a lioness.*

My response to my friend's question had provoked something in me. I found the image of 'attentive stillness' utterly compelling. And it brought sudden clarity to how I was feeling about the distraction and busyness of my life – a clarity for which I had been searching for many years. It seemed to describe an entirely different way of living. Instead of inviting God into my day and then heading off at full tilt, I could approach the day with a different mindset. I could take time to be attentive to God's presence in the midst of the demands of the day, and then allow my activity to flow from that place of stillness, love and peace.

As I looked deeper into the image of the lioness, my editor, Stephanie, suggested I look at a book that I remember from my childhood. I remembered it being made into a wonderful film (with a catchy theme tune which I have since discovered people of a certain age can't help but sing when you mention the name!). The book is called *Born Free*.

It's a story based on the experience of Joy and George Adamson, who worked as game wardens in Kenya. It is a wonderful account of how they rescued three baby lion cubs, just four days old. Two were taken to a zoo in Holland where they were cared for, but the smallest, Elsa, they kept.

The Adamsons raised Elsa by hand in their own home for four years. Even as a fully grown lioness, she would sleep on a camp bed next to them and, such was the love and respect that grew between them, they were often woken by her rough tongue licking their faces. There have been other true stories of wild cats being raised in captivity, but the ground-breaking part of this story is that Joy and George were eventually able to return Elsa to the wild. She was not only able to go back to her homeland, but to integrate with a pride and raise cubs of her own. However, the bond of friendship between them was so strong that Elsa came back lovingly every time Joy and George visited her territory. She had the best of both worlds.

As I read the book, I realized that there was much I could learn from Elsa the lioness. Not only is she the inspiration for the title of both Joy's book and mine, but the invitations to live differently all arise from her way of living.

In one of the most quoted passages from Eugene Peterson's *The Message* translation of the Bible, Jesus said to his followers:

> *'Are you tired? Worn out? Burned out on religion? Come to me. Get away with me and you'll recover your life. I'll show you how to take a real rest. Walk with me and work with me – watch how I do it. Learn the unforced rhythms of grace. I won't lay anything heavy or ill-fitting on you. Keep company with me and you'll learn to live freely and lightly.'*
>
> MATTHEW 11:28–30 (MSG)

In an equally familiar but more traditional version of the same passage, Jesus says:

> *'Come to me, all you who are weary and burdened, and I will give you rest. Take my yoke upon you and learn from me, for I am gentle and humble in heart, and you will find rest for your souls. For my yoke is easy and my burden is light.'*
>
> MATTHEW 11:28–30 (NIV)

The significance of this familiar imagery can sometimes be lost on us today, particularly if we live in an urban setting. My daughter and son-in-law are farmers, and when I spend time with them, I am often reminded of how Jesus grounded so much of his teaching in the context of the first-century agrarian society that was so familiar to him and his followers. The image Jesus gives here is of the yoke, a wooden frame or crossbar used to link two oxen as they dragged farming equipment across the fields. A poorly fitting yoke would be a burden; a well-fitting yoke would lighten the load.

The word 'easy' is a translation of the Greek word *chrestos*, and it can also mean 'good', 'benevolent', 'agreeable', or even 'effective'. So Jesus' offer of an 'easy' yoke is in direct contrast to his stern words about the Pharisees. Speaking to the crowds and his disciples, Jesus said:

> *'The teachers of the law and the Pharisees sit in Moses' seat. So you must be careful to do everything they tell you. But do not do what they do, for they do not practise what they preach. They tie up heavy, cumbersome loads and put them on other people's shoulders, but they themselves are not willing to lift a finger to move them.'*

MATTHEW 23:2–4

The 'heavy … loads' Jesus refers to are the Pharisees' interpretations of and additions to the yoke of the Torah. In their desire to keep people from sin, they had added rule upon rule, regulation upon regulation, so that keeping it had become a cumbersome and onerous load. No matter how hard they tried to keep the Law they would be exhausted by the burden.

In contrast, Jesus fulfilled the law completely in himself. And the yoke he offers us is an easy one that brings us freedom and life. Pastor and author Dane Ortlund comments:

> Whether you are actively working hard to crowbar your life into smoothness ('labour') or passively finding yourself weighed down by something outside your control ('heavy laden'), Jesus Christ's desire that you find rest … outstrips even your own.[4]

The symbolism of the easy yoke is not meant to give us the impression that effort plays no part in following him. But Jesus invites us to come to him, learn from him, and to work from a place of rest.

The easy yoke involves both work and grace – effort alongside life in the Spirit.

God, in his kindness, has twice spoken to me about the

---

4 Dane C. Ortlund, *Gentle and Lowly: The Heart of Christ for Sinners and Sufferers* (Crossway Books, 2020), p21.

significance of these verses for my life. The first was many years ago, when a friend described a scene in his mind's eye: a picture of me struggling to carry a piece of roughly hewn wood across my shoulders. The yoke was uncomfortable and ill-fitting; it rubbed, causing blisters, and bits of wood were giving me splinters. But as he stayed with the image, the wood began to change and gradually become a beautiful, honed, well-fitting piece of mahogany that was a joy to wear. As my friend spoke, I sensed that this image was God speaking directly into my life. If I could lean into the story and learn to work with the grain of the universe, falling in step with Jesus' purpose and pace for my life, gradually, I would trade the ill-fitting yoke of a hurried existence for a well-fitting one that would enable me to 'walk with' and 'work with' Jesus, 'living freely and lightly', and better reflecting his image to those around me.

More recently, Richard and I signed up to attend an online conference. We watched from the comfort of our home, and as part of the event, we found ourselves whisked into a Zoom breakout room and invited to pray across the screen with a small group, most of whom we'd never met before. There were no claps of thunder or lights in the sky heralding a holy moment, but as we prayed, a friend shared an image that spoke into our lives, once again based on Jesus' words in Matthew 11. He described a giant metronome, keeping a steady rhythmic beat. But instead of marking regular time for a piano recital, this metronome towered over the hustle and bustle of a town square. Here it was again, walking in step with Jesus, right in the mundanity of everyday life. Even in the heart of the commerce and busyness of the town square, it was possible to have a steady rhythm.

My experience over the years and that of saints down the generations is that when God says something more than once, it is wise to pay attention. Recalling this, I knew that I needed to ask some questions, beginning with what lay behind my 'ant-like' behaviour. I figured that, like a good doctor, I needed not just to look at the symptoms, but to ask what was causing my busy way of living in the first place. I needed to step back and put the little ant under a microscope.

PAUSE TO CONSIDER:

- *What animal best represents the way you are living life at the moment?*
- *If you could be any other animal, which one would you like to be?*

CHAPTER 2

MAKING EVERY SECOND COUNT!

She hunts when her environment is most favourable – at dusk and pre-dawn. No one can rush a sunset or delay the sun's rise, so lionesses are patient and intentional.[5]

My friend's simple question: 'What animal would you like to be?' had certainly brought me a moment of clarity, but my longing to discover a different way of living had begun many years before. In fact, as I started to put the little ant under the microscope, I can see that it went as far back as my childhood.

When poet William Wordsworth wrote that 'the child is the father of the man',[6] he meant that the character traits that are formed in us as children stay with us into adult life. It is not just unconscious mannerisms or idiosyncratic turns of phrase that become part of our personality, but deeper, unconscious patterns of behaviour, including those we adopt to help us navigate challenging times.

My life is no exception. Looking back, I can identify some formative seasons that reinforced my natural tendency to live life in the fast lane. As a child, I was the responsible eldest of four, which meant that I had three ready-made playmates to cajole, coax and corral into endless hours of play. Research shows that our place in the order of the family has a bearing on our development,[7] and as the big sister, I was in charge. As long as I can remember, I have

5 Lisa Bevere, *Lioness Arising: Wake Up and Change Your World* (Waterbrook Press, 2011), p132.
6 William Wordsworth, *Poems in Two Volumes, Vol. II* (Project Gutenberg, 2005), p34.
7 Sandra E. Black, Erik Grönqvist, Björn Öckert, 'Born to Lead? The Effect of Birth Order on Noncognitive Abilities', *The Review of Economics and Statistics* (2018) 100 (2), pp274–286.

been a leader, carrying a sense of what needs doing and stepping up to what I believed was my job to make happen.

Life changed when I went to boarding school at the age of ten; my time was no longer my own. The belief that 'the devil finds work for idle hands to do' meant that resourceful timetabling kept us occupied every second of the day, including evenings and weekends. As a result, much activity and little space just to 'be' became a normal way to live.

Fast forward a number of years and I found myself sitting in the swanky reception area of the up-and-coming law firm where I had landed my first job as a newly qualified solicitor. I was shown to my desk and introduced to someone who was to be my constant companion, at my side every second of the day: my timesheet. This was a piece of A4 paper on which I was to record my billable hours. Lawyers earn a living by charging for their time, and so every six-minute unit of my day had to be allocated to a particular file and recorded on a grid. Walking to the coffee machine, chatting to a colleague by the water fountain, or even visiting the loo were all to be accounted as 'NCT' (non-chargeable time). There were no worthy statements of office values in the reception area – or even in the lift – but if there had been, I imagine that adorning the walls would have been the mantra 'Make every second count!'

While this may not be a bad sentiment for an ambitious law firm, and time recording is an efficient way of running a business, there was also a shadow side. Imposing this rigid framework over every minute of my working day reinforced my propensity to measure 'success' in terms of busyness, productivity and achievement. Wanting to impress, I set out to 'make every second count' the only way I knew how: by keeping my foot on the accelerator. I flew from activity to activity and my action-packed week had very little down time.

As a child, I remember being on the edge of my seat watching the plate-spinner perform his act at Billy Smart's Circus. The idea was for him to keep an increasing number of plates spinning on the ends of long poles. It was vital to keep them going at the same velocity; if any of the plates slowed down too much, they would crash to the floor, smashing into a thousand pieces. The excitement of the audience mounted as the performer added more and more plates, frantically dashing to and fro, constantly evaluating which plates were fine and which were heading for disaster. It was fun to watch – but is exhausting as a way to live.

The season of life that we are in, our unique responsibilities and God-given capacity, mean that the pressures we face will weigh differently on each one of us. But, however well we appear to carry out our responsibilities, fault lines in our character can combine with our schedules and lead us to live our lives overstretched, running to keep still, or simply feeling stressed, anxious and weary. Some of us are better at hiding it than others, but for most of us there will come a time when we recognize the undercurrents that are driving our schedules.

As I was to discover, even self-appointed Superwoman has her limitations. Little did I know it, but overnight, my full and busy schedule was about to hit the buffers. In the early years of marriage, an accident left me with a broken pelvis, and I was faced with lying on my back for weeks on end. All of a sudden, all that 'make it happen' drive and activity counted for nothing. I wasn't able to run between the poles and keep the plates spinning. There were no timesheets to complete to justify my existence. All the metrics of success that I'd come to rely on were no longer there, only an enforced pause. I couldn't even make myself a cup of tea. It was as if, for the first time in my life, I had the time and space to pause … and to think.

On the bookshelf was the wonderful *Chronicles of Narnia* series by C.S. Lewis which I had enjoyed when growing up, and I decided to reach out to this old friend. As I turned the pages, the black and white illustrations and the smell of the timeworn paper took me straight back to my childhood, and over the next few weeks, I accompanied the Pevensie children on their adventures in the magical land of Narnia. I fell in love again with Aslan and discovered more of his 'deep magic'. Simply stopping and having time was a gift. And with all the activity and busyness of life on hold, my heart had the time and space to rest and be captivated by what Lewis calls 'that other country':

> I must keep alive in myself the desire for my true country, which I shall not find till after death; I must never let it get snowed under or turned aside; I must make it the main object of life to press on to that other country and to help others to do the same.[8]

In those months of enforced rest and stillness, I caught a glimpse of that country on the horizon. But with my recovery came a return to normal life. As a black-suited, kitten-heeled lawyer by day, a denim-clad, music-loving, coffee-drinking youth group leader by night, and the 'hostess-with-the-mostest' at weekends, I made every second count. The arrival of children saw the kitten heels exchanged for trainers and the black suit for a banana-stained T-shirt, but essentially the pace of life remained the same. In the years that followed, what the Bible calls the 'worries of life' (Mark 4:19), aka all that is involved in parenting four lively children, Saturday sports fixtures, school parents' evenings, searching for missing hamsters and swimming goggles, all while fighting the losing battle of a half-tidy house, were making their presence felt. The pile of plates that I needed to keep spinning seemed to be growing exponentially. At that time, I was church warden of a big Anglican church, a role which required not only time and energy but considerable emotional and spiritual investment. I had pressed the pause button on my role as a solicitor, but I was hearing cases and seeking to deliver justice as a magistrate. This, together with time to be with family and friends, all combined to mean that the pursuit of that 'other country' was easily 'snowed under'.

8 C.S. Lewis, *Mere Christianity* (Geoffrey Bles, 1952), pp135–137.

Putting on a hero's cape means you can cover a lot of ground and get stuff done. But as time went on, I began to have a nagging feeling that my outward productivity was a smokescreen for an inner restlessness, and that there had to be something more. Multi-tasking gave the illusion that I could achieve and perform well, without giving my full attention to anything. On the surface, everything was good and worthwhile – there was just too much of it. Life was wide but not very deep. Ironically, 'getting stuff done' included putting practices in place to grow in my faith – but everything seemed to stay at a superficial level. As I read the Bible, I didn't notice words like 'efficiency' or even 'productivity' describing the way of Jesus.

It was an insignificant request from a friend that shone a spotlight on the condition of my heart. After a full day, Richard and I also had plans for the evening and although the turnaround was tight, we could manage it. Just as we were about to leave the house, a friend called. Her car had broken down and she needed a lift to the garage. She was a good friend and I wanted to help, but in that moment I felt conflicted. Instead of adjusting my priorities and delaying the evening's plans, I hesitated. In that moment of indecision God held a mirror to my interior world. And I didn't like what I saw.

It was as if I was looking at the motivation of my heart with new eyes. When unexpected requests or unforeseen demands interrupted my day, I knew my default was to feel irritated and resentful. I longed to be less self-centred and more loving. To put the needs of others before my desires, to know more of God, and to experience more of his love and peace. But the pace of my life didn't seem to leave much room for change.

Author Emilie Griffin describes so well how I was feeling at the time:

Times come when we yearn for more of God than our schedules will allow. We are tired, we are crushed, we are crowded by friends and acquaintances, commitments and obligations. The life of grace is abounding, but we are too busy for it! Even good obligations begin to hem us in.[9]

Paul writes to the Christians in Galatia: 'It is for freedom that Christ has set us free. Stand firm, then, and do not let yourselves be burdened again by a yoke of slavery' (Galatians 5:1). I wanted that freedom. I wanted to be the kind of person who could spend time in God's presence, without the distractions and demands of the day crashing in, who was interruptible, who readily responded to the needs of others in love. I resolved to rationalize the family diary, take less on, and to be more deliberate, more present and more considered in how I lived my life. But it was to take a quarter of a century and the impact of a world pandemic for those resolutions finally to make the eighteen-inch journey from my head to my heart.

PAUSE TO CONSIDER:

- *What experiences in your past have shaped the pace at which you live your life now?*

- *Have you sensed any whispers or nudges of an invitation to live life differently?*

---

9 Emilie Griffin, *Wilderness Time: A Guide for Spiritual Retreat* (Harper Collins, 1997), p1.

CHAPTER 3

A *KAIROS* MOMENT

> On the morning after our arrival we started our programme. First we took off her collar, as the symbol of liberation.[10]

Author Juliet Funt described so perfectly what I was experiencing:

> There's no "they" doing it to us anymore. From corporate executive to sheep farmer to retiree, our driving pace and pressure have become fully *internalized*. We carry it with us wherever we go. But as indoctrinated as most of us are to the white-water rush of busyness, a small yearning lurks within: A little whisper we can hardly hear says we just need a minute to think – a minute to breathe. And sometimes we get a hint of it by accident.[11]

That hint was about to become a clarion call: Covid-19 hit the world. Individual circumstances undoubtedly made a big difference to people's experience of living through the pandemic. Valiant home-schooling parents tackled the impossible task of juggling spellings, Shakespeare and science, all the while managing their inbox and the family Xbox. Some people suffered acute loneliness. Job security was on the line, family finances were stretched, and many suffered bereavement and loss. Across the board, our mental wellbeing took a huge hit. And I saw first-hand in the lives of my own children the unbelievable weight that frontline workers carried as they continued to serve our communities. But for all the grief, trauma and stress, there were also glimpses of what the Bible calls 'treasures

---

10 Joy Adamson, *Born Free* (Pantheon Books, 1960), p76.
11 Juliet Funt, *A Minute to Think: Reclaim Creativity, Conquer Busyness, and Do Your Best Work* (HarperBus, 2021), p16.

… in the darkness' (Isaiah 45:3, NLT) – insights that we would not have discovered without those unbelievably difficult times.

One day when I was chatting to a friend about this, she used a phrase that caught my attention. She spoke of a 'liminal space' – a waiting area between one point in time and space and the next, a threshold between the old season and the new. I believe Covid-19 catapulted all of us into such a space, unsettling routines and forcing us to realign our priorities; to think about what things are important to us. For some this may be a welcome opportunity, while others may be mourning a happier pre-pandemic way of life. Lamenting what we have lost is important, but in time, whatever our situation, we may recognize that out of the pandemic comes an invitation to recalibrate our lives.

Of necessity, Covid-19 made us slow down. In some ways, I realized that I had relied on the adrenaline rush and energy of my fast-paced lifestyle to propel me forward, but the restrictions of lockdown presented an opportunity to rediscover a new way of living, one that had sometimes been so close but always slipped away.

I order the same calendar every year which takes pride of place in our kitchen. When our children were growing up and had schedules of their own, the calendar was the motherboard of our family life. Dire consequences were threatened for anyone who failed to write an appointment on the calendar, particularly if it affected numbers for meals, and woe betide the person who wrote on it with a fat, luminous pink marker rather than the regulation fine black Sharpie!

Before the pandemic, each month there would have been thirty squares, jam-packed with diary entries: speaking engagements, filming dates, work meetings, event tours, church gatherings, sports events, dental appointments, hospital check-ups, haircuts or coffee with friends. But then along came Covid.

It was a Sunday evening at the end of May and the UK had been in lockdown for almost two months. Countless trips, events and coffee dates had been cancelled already. But when I turned the page to look at the following month, my heart skipped a beat. Thirty white spaces greeted me.

At one level, there was so much I missed: meeting up with family and friends, worshipping with our church family, the camaraderie of the workplace, listening to podcasts on my commute to the office, the adrenaline rush that was part and parcel of our Care for the Family road tours, the immense privilege of speaking to families, and even the all-inclusive breakfast and good night guarantee at our much-loved Premier Inns. But there was something about that white space that beckoned to me: it offered me time and space to slow down and an opportunity to be present to others, to myself and to God.

I identified with author Henri Nouwen who, looking at his busy lifestyle, wrote:

> I started to see how much I had indeed fallen in love with my own compulsions and illusions, and how much I needed to step back and wonder, 'Is there a quiet stream underneath the fluctuating affirmations and rejections of my little world? Is there a still point where my life is anchored and from which I can reach out with hope and courage and confidence?'[12]

In graphic design, white space is an area without print. In business, it suggests room to manoeuvre in a crowded playing field. Authors use white space to help the reader process information. And in the context of mental wellbeing, white space represents a moment of calm. Juliet Funt refers to white space as 'time with no assignment ... the open, unscheduled time – long or short, planned or improvised – that is accessed by taking a strategic pause in the activities of life.'[13] It is a pause, not just to down tools and do nothing, but to

---

12 Henry J.M. Nouwen, *The Genesee Diary: Report from a Trappist Monastery* (Doubleday, 1989), pxii.
13 Juliet Funt, *A Minute to Think: Reclaim Creativity, Conquer Busyness, and Do Your Best Work* (HarperBus, 2021), p16.

intentionally create space for a different kind of stillness. In fact, it is the very opposite to the way I had lived much of my life.

During the pandemic, many people had to work harder than they'd ever worked before. But for others like me, the lockdown forced us to slow down and gave us the opportunity for that strategic pause. And then little by little, vaccination by vaccination, discarded mask by discarded mask, and with the ever-decreasing length of social distancing, lockdown ended. Was I grateful? Of course. But I also felt a strange emotion – loss. The pandemic had given me the chance to live differently. I had crossed the Rubicon … and I didn't want to go back.

Of course, I was looking forward to returning to some kind of normality, but could I preserve the gift the pandemic had given me – that white space? As restrictions lifted, the demands of life began to pile back on, taking no prisoners. The black Sharpie returned to doing what it does best – filling in the calendar squares. And I began to wonder if living at a different pace was even possible. My busy ant-like behaviour seemed to be my default, and the attentive stillness of the lioness now seemed a pipe dream away.

The Bible uses the Greek word *kairos* to mean an extraordinary moment or appointed time in the purposes of God that invites a response. We read in Mark's gospel:

> *After John was put in prison, Jesus went into Galilee, proclaiming the good news of God. 'The time has come,' he said. 'The kingdom of God has come near. Repent and believe the good news!'*

MARK 1:14–15

The word used for 'The time' here is *kairos*. Writing to Titus, Paul uses the same word: 'And now at just the right time he has revealed this message' (Titus 1:3, NLT). It is a qualitative time, where all the right conditions are in place for change.

Throughout history there have been pivotal *kairos* moments that have shaped nations, movements, communities and individual lives. Dr Martin Luther King Jr's 'I Have a Dream' speech galvanized the civil rights movement in America, the First World War ushered in societal and cultural change, and more recently Steve Jobs' introduction of the smartphone changed our relationship with technology. These, and many other events like them, can all be seen as *kairos* moments – including the impact of the Covid-19 global pandemic. Author Arundhati Roy speaks of how 'historically, pandemics have forced humans to break with the past and imagine their world anew. This one is no different. It is a portal, a gateway between one world and the next.'[14]

The experience of lockdown had ushered in my own *kairos* moment and the opportunity for change. The challenge was how to grasp it.

PAUSE TO CONSIDER:

- *Can you identify any possible still points, white space or potential pauses in the day or week ahead?*

- *What treasure did you discover in the pandemic or during any other periods of darkness you have experienced?*

---

14 Arundhati Roy: 'The pandemic is a portal', *Financial Times*, 3 April 2020, ft.com (accessed 25 February 2023).

CHAPTER 4

THE HEART OF THE MATTER

> In order for … lionesses to roar they must change their posture. Their powerful heads drop and they expand their chests in order to fill their lungs with air.[15]

Could I change from the busy little ant to a still, yet purposeful, lioness? Is a change of that nature even possible? Or is it simply a money-spinning concept conjured up by the self-improvement gurus who speak into our culture, offering no shortage of ideas to help you to become the best version of yourself? As good as some of their suggestions are, they only go so far – mainly because they require us to 'fix' ourselves with yet more activity. I knew that simply adding creative ideas to an already full schedule was not going to be the solution.

One of my children's favourite stories was Eric Carle's award-winning book *The Very Hungry Caterpillar*. The story charts the little caterpillar's progress as he eats his way through the week. On Monday he eats one apple, on Tuesday, two pears and on each succeeding day he eats more and more, culminating in a smörgåsbord of food on Saturday. Full to bursting, he climbs inside the cocoon, stays there for three weeks, and on the final page he emerges as a beautiful butterfly. His DNA is the same, but he's a different creature altogether. No amount of studying, hard work and discipline, clever tricks or financial investment on the little caterpillar's behalf could bring about that transformation. His part was simply to create the right environment, to weave the cocoon, to stay inside and then to allow this fundamental change to take place.

The word 'metamorphosis' (the process of changing into something completely different) has its roots in the Greek word *metamorphoō*. And this is the word Paul uses in his letter to the

15 Lisa Bevere, *Lioness Arising: Wake Up and Change Your World* (Waterbrook Press, 2011), p205.

Romans when he writes: 'Do not be conformed to this world, but be transformed by the renewal of your mind' (Romans 12:2, ESV). Reflecting on this process, author Ruth Haley Barton says that:

> ... the process of spiritual transformation [is] squarely in the category that we call mystery – something outside the range of normal human activity and understanding that can be grasped only through divine revelation and brought about by divine activity ... It is one thing to be able to tweak and control external behaviors; it is another thing to experience those internal seismic shifts that change the way I exist in this world – from a worm crawling on my belly to a butterfly winging its way to the sky. *That* kind of change is something only God can do.[16]

No amount of pulling ourselves up by our bootstraps, self-help podcasts, HIIT exercise regimes, time management gizmos or Tippex on the kitchen calendar can bring about deep transformation in our lives. At the end of the day, transformation is God's work. Our role is to weave the cocoon, that is, to create the environment in which change can take place and craft opportunities where we can give our hearts access to the transforming work of the Holy Spirit. That 'cocoon' can look different for each one of us, but it begins with our desire for change.

Jane, a young mother, described what had happened to kick-start this change in her:

> *'Looking back I can see that God was gently allowing what I now call a "holy discontent" to rise up within me. After having my son, I joined a toddler group at church, and as I made friends I became more and more aware of the gap between my experience of faith and theirs. Their relationship with God seemed colourful, whereas mine felt grey and boring. I prayed that God would bring about change in my life. I began to read the Bible, I opened up to friends about my disappointment with my faith and tried to hang out with people whose faith I*

16 Ruth Haley Barton, *Sacred Rhythms: Arranging Our Lives for Spiritual Transformation* (InterVarsity Press, 2006), p12.

admired, in the hope it would rub off on me. It hasn't happened overnight, and I have a long way to go, but I know God is using those places and people to change my heart.'

For others the desire for transformational change can come as a result of challenging times. In the Sermon on the Mount, Jesus explains why: 'You're blessed when you're at the end of your rope. With less of you there is more of God and his rule' (Matthew 5:3, MSG).

Malc's experience of the transforming work of God in his life came in the context of the breakdown of his marriage. He said:

'I should have seen the signs but I just didn't see it coming. I felt such a failure. I was at rock bottom and in my desperation cried out to God. He used this low time in my life, when I had nothing left, to bring me back into a deeper relationship with him.'

Change begins with our heart. When the Bible speaks of the heart, it doesn't refer to the fluffy red and pink hearts that adorn Hallmark cards and balloons on Valentine's Day. Rather than being a symbol of the centre of our emotions, it is what author Dane Ortlund calls 'our motivational headquarters'.[17] He writes:

The heart, in biblical terms, is not part of who we are but the center of who we are. Our heart is what defines and directs us … The heart is a matter of life. It is what makes us the human being each of us is. The heart drives all we do. It is who we are.[18]

Our heart is the place of intimacy, the place where we can know and be known, love and be loved. It is a place of love. And perhaps most of all in this context, it is a place of rest and of freedom.

Much has been written over the years about the process of spiritual transformation, but way back in the fifth century, St Augustine captured the essence of the matter in just less than a hundred characters – words that pack a punch and could form the

17 Dane C. Ortlund, *Gentle and Lowly: The Heart of Christ for Sinners and Sufferers* (Crossway Books, 2020), p18.
18 Ibid. pp18–19.

basis of a fantastic tweet. In his autobiography, *The Confessions*, he wrote: 'You have made us for yourself, O Lord, and our hearts are restless until they find their rest in You.'[19]

In one of my favourite psalms, the warrior King David spoke of the attitude that is needed if we are to find that rest:

My heart is not proud, LORD,
my eyes are not haughty;
I do not concern myself with great matters
or things too wonderful for me.
But I have calmed and quieted my soul
I am like a weaned child with its mother;
like a weaned child I am content.
Israel, put your hope in the LORD
both now and forevermore.

PSALM 131

I love the way that, although he was a soldier, David chose to place these verses in everyday family life, and I have returned to them often, picturing a mother cradling a tiny newborn baby satisfied from a feed, held safe and secure. But one day it struck me: I'd missed the point entirely! This child *isn't* a helpless newborn, dependent on its mother for its every need. He is weaned – a toddler or even older. When Hannah handed Samuel to Eli's care, he is also described as being 'weaned' (1 Samuel 1:23–24). The child in the Psalm knows the contentment and security of his mother's lap, but he has agency. He can choose to climb onto her lap or play elsewhere. He knows how to get his needs met, where to go, and how to be at rest. He knows how to quieten and still his soul.

Charles Spurgeon wrote of this psalm: 'It is one of the shortest Psalms to read, but one of the longest to learn. It speaks of a young child, but it contains the experience of a man [or woman] in Christ.'[20]

19 Saint Augustine of Hippo, *The Confessions of St Augustine* (Doubleday, 1960), p43.
20 Charles H. Spurgeon, *Charles Spurgeon's Classics* (Pronoun, 2016), p6163.

Perhaps one of the reasons that this is a lifelong lesson is the bias of our human heart to sin. And during the pandemic the state of our hearts was magnified on a global scale, as political and racial conflict, war, and civil unrest were exposed on the world stage.

A friend who is an Anglican minister in a busy London church recently spoke to me about how his experience of the pandemic had brought him face to face with his humanity.

'During lockdown we were living in a small London flat with our children, the demands of ministry were relentless. I was burning the candle at both ends, I wasn't taking a day off, or getting enough sleep. I was irritable with my wife and children, and on more than one occasion lost my temper with colleagues and even with members of the church family. I felt disappointed in myself. As I reflected on Jesus' words that 'out of the overflow of the heart the mouth speaks' (Matthew 12:34) it was sobering for me to realize that the pressure of Covid had exposed what was really in my heart.

One of the joys of my job is to preach, and on many occasions I have found that as I have prepared my talk Scripture has held a mirror to my life, and I realize I am preaching to an audience of one. Instead of sinking into despair about the state of my heart, I (and others) needed a message of hope. Like any good sermon, the message came with alliteration! I needed to remember that not only have we been saved from the penalty of sin, but we are daily being saved from the power of sin. And one day we will be saved from the presence of sin. We are a work in progress.'

This is good news!

Gary Haugen is the founder of International Justice Mission (IJM), an organization that seeks to protect the poor from violence and injustice in the developing world. Those who fight injustice know it can be a stressful and often a dangerous role. Such is the pressure on the staff at IJM that Gary has introduced intentional rhythms of spiritual formation for the organization, and in particular thirty minutes of stillness at the start of the working day. He believes this practice will help his staff work not from a place of anxiety or anger, but from a place of peace and closeness with the Father.

What could it look like in our pressured or distracted existence at home or in the workplace to create the space for the Holy Spirit to bring about the necessary change in our lives, so that we live from that place of love and intimacy, rest and contentment? Later chapters explore this in more depth, but for me the starting point is to find simple ways of being more aware of God's presence in the every day. It could be by inviting God into my day each morning, or when I sit down at my desk; going for a walk and taking time to notice the frost on the branches, the drops of water on the leaves, or the clouds racing across the sky; creating playlists of my favourite music; inviting God into my writing or to a meeting; listening to an inspiring podcast on my commute; enjoying a flat white in a café with only my journal as company (my idea of heaven!); having a candlelit bath; meeting with friends to pray; or remembering to be thankful at night.

These are not formulas or mechanisms for spiritual formation, but they simply create the opportunity for us to spend time in God's presence, looking to him to bring about change in our lives. In fact, if transformation is God's work perhaps one of the most important things we can do is to pray – to ask God to do what only he can do. Theologian John Webster captures this well:

> Prayer is that basic human action which corresponds to our incapacity, to our unsuitability for what is required of us, and therefore to the utter necessity of the merciful intervention of God.[21]

Proverbs tells us that it all begins with the heart: 'Above all else, guard your heart, for everything you do flows from it' (Proverbs 4:23). The things we love and pay attention to are the wellspring from which our lives flow.

Philosopher James K.A. Smith captures this truth in the title of his bestselling book, *You Are What You Love*. He explains that the people and things we love and worship fundamentally shape our hearts and direct our lives. In addressing the possibility of change, he writes:

21 John Webster, *The Culture of Theology* (Baker Publishing Group, 2019), p143.

We can't recalibrate the heart from the top down, through merely informational measures. The orientation of the heart happens from the bottom up, through the formation of our habits of desire. Learning to love [God] takes practice.[22]

So while this is God's work, it seems that we also have a part to play in changing the orientation of our hearts. We can choose to take time to discover habits, routines and rhythms that work in our season of life and suit our personality. Practices that help us grasp liberating truths about God and about ourselves give us the best chance of experiencing the Holy Spirit's activity and transforming presence in our lives.

But before we rush to download the app that promises free, next-day-delivery spiritual maturity, it's worth reminding ourselves of three things.

Firstly, this journey is not for the fainthearted. Maybe we shouldn't be too surprised at how hard it is to not only discover an attentive stillness like that of the lioness but to maintain it for more than a short period. I can picture her under a tree in the evening light, her young gathered around her, resting but fully alert, present to the moment, calm but able to jump up at a moment's notice. And able to stay in that place for hours.

Secondly, this is not just a matter of a few New Year's resolutions. In his letter to the Ephesian church, the apostle Paul warns us that we are in a spiritual battle and encourages us to prepare ourselves:

Put on the full armour of God, so that you can take your stand against the devil's schemes. For our struggle is not against flesh and blood, but against the rulers, against the authorities, against the powers of this dark world and against the spiritual forces of evil in the heavenly realms.

EPHESIANS 6:11-12

---

22 James K.A. Smith, *You Are What You Love: The Spiritual Power of Habit* (Brazos Press, 2016), p25.

There are no quick-fix, instant solutions. Programmes, skills, methods and techniques alone, however diligently followed, will not 'achieve' transformation. This is a spiritual battle.

Finally, we must debunk any assumption that we are in the driving seat in our relationship with God. Our spiritual life is a journey. Or, to borrow the title of a book by Eugene Peterson, it is 'a long obedience in the same direction.' Author Robert Mulholland reminds us that:

> … the way to spiritual wholeness is seen to lie in an increasingly faithful response to the One whose purpose shapes our paths, whose grace redeems our detours, whose power liberates us from the crippling bondages of the prior journey and whose transforming presence meets us at each turn in the road. In other words, holistic spirituality is a pilgrimage of deepening responsiveness to God's control of our life and being.[23]

Mulholland calls us to a new journey and in the second part of this book, we will look at twelve ways to walk that road – and in particular, some lessons we can learn from the lioness.

PAUSE TO CONSIDER:

- *What could create an environment that would make it more possible for God to carry out his transforming work in you?*

- *What is it that motivates you at the moment, and what do you give your attention to most?*

- *Where would you like to turn your attention?*

---

23 M. Robert Mulholland Jr., *Invitation to a Journey: A Roadmap for Spiritual Formation* (InterVarsity Press, 2016), p16.

PART TWO

THE LIONESS ON THE HORIZON

12 LESSONS FROM THE PLAINS

CHAPTER 5

HAVING NOTHING TO PROVE

> Not only do lionesses innately know what they are capable of and how to do what they do well ... but their lives are relatively uncomplicated. They rest when tired and hunt and eat when they are hungry. Outside of that, they mainly play![24]

It was my first day at boarding school. The journey seemed to have taken an age, but finally there I was, standing on the steps, waving goodbye to my family. In my left hand I held my bag and in my right hand, my teddy bear. I was ten years old.

I watched the tail lights of the car disappear down the drive and taking a deep breath, went inside to this strange new world. My heart pounding, I surveyed a room of girls who all looked as nervous as me. We all knew the unwritten subtext: we had to make this work; there was no Plan B. Like it or lump it, we would be doing life together for the next seven years.

Later that night, I lay in my bed in the darkness and wondered what the next day would bring. I held my teddy close; he was a shabby little bear with much of his fur loved off. Just as I was drifting off to sleep, Mrs Ashcroft, the matron, put her head around the door. 'Girls,' she said. 'Sarah in the next room is crying because she's missing home. I wondered if anyone might have a spare teddy she could borrow?'

I agonized for a moment, but it didn't take me long to decide. As I handed over my precious bear, I felt the warm glow of satisfaction that often comes with a sacrificial act of giving. I felt sad for Sarah

24 Lisa Bevere, *Lioness Arising: Wake Up and Change Your World* (Waterbrook Press, 2011), p153.

and was pleased my teddy might bring her some comfort. But in that split second, something else happened, something much deeper, something I would not be aware of for decades: I made the unconscious decision that I was never going to be Sarah. I would never admit to missing home or be vulnerable enough to say I needed a teddy.

I put on the strong, protective armour of self-sufficiency which served me well, and I set out to prove myself to my new friends, to the school, and to my parents. My ten-year-old ambition over the next seven years was to achieve three things: to earn a much-coveted place in the school choir, a place in the 1st team for sports, and most of all, a place in the hallowed 'Study One' – home to the Head Girl, Deputy Head Girl and Captain of Games. And over the years that followed, I set my mind to that task and did it well. I achieved everything on my bucket list. And it felt so good.

Perhaps, as a way to help navigate the challenges of boarding school, it wasn't a bad strategy. But as I came to discover, living in that well-worn groove as a twenty-, thirty-, forty-, even fifty-something is not sustainable. In fact, it often caused me to burn the candle at both ends. As a young lawyer, I'd rehearse my performance until the early hours the night before a hearing. As a young mother, I'd stay up way too late to put the finishing touches to birthday cakes or World Book Day costumes. And, perhaps ironically, I'd set the alarm super early to make sure that the first and most important thing on my to-do list – my early morning quiet time – was also completed to my satisfaction.

The truth is that whether we are aged ten or a hundred and ten, many of us spend our lives relying on performance to prove our worth – and I love the way that the Psalms address this bias of the human heart. Psalm 46 begins: 'God is our refuge and strength, an ever-present help in trouble', reminding us that no amount of striving and effort can resolve the big issues of the world. The psalmist writes in dramatic terms of nations in uproar, kingdoms falling and mountains falling into the sea, but there follows a wonderful verse reminding us of our place in the universe: 'Be still' (verse 10). One translation hits the nail on the head exactly: 'Stop striving and know that I am God' (Psalm 46:10, NASB). He is God and we are not.

As a newly qualified solicitor, the best training came from working alongside those with more experience, and so it was that I found myself sharing an office with one of the company's high flyers. Before the days of email, correspondence took the form of dictated letters, and as a newbie my letters had to be vetted by a senior lawyer before being sent out. This man was a stickler for detail; a missing capital letter or misplaced comma meant that the letter was rejected and sent back for retyping. The mantra he drummed into me, and that he would have had tattooed across his forehead if he'd had a chance, was 'The Pursuit of Excellence'.

While this maxim can be an indicator of good client service, it can cause us to lose our way, breeding a performance mentality in us with regard to the whole of life. Looking back, it was this deep-rooted need to achieve and excel that propelled me across the finishing tape in the mothers' race, saw me relegating my sunken Victoria sponge or less-than-perfect chocolate brownies to the bin, and even drove me to rehearse eloquent prayers for the student committee prayer meeting.

The adrenaline rush of success and achievement massages our ego and appeals to our sense of importance, so that gradually we come to believe that our worth and value lies in what we do. Living *for* rather than *from* approval, we find ourselves responding to an exhausting litany of 'oughts' and 'shoulds', and before we know it, we are tethered to this powerful source of identity and worth.

A part of my job that I enjoy is the opportunity to engage in discussion programmes on the radio. One lively debate that will stay forever in my memory was sparked during an interview with broadcaster Vanessa Phelps on BBC Radio London. I was invited to take part in a debate on the back of an article in the *Evening Standard* newspaper where I had advised parents to reassure children that 'It's OK to be ordinary'. Taken out of context, this is a difficult concept to grasp – as parents, of course we want our children to succeed, to be the best they can be – so it provoked a heated discussion on air. But my context for this controversial statement was the tsunami of anxiety that has overwhelmed a generation; in particular, a culture where TikTok videos, Instagram reels and reality TV have turned the ordinary into the extraordinary every day of the week. Singing, dancing, baking, and even falling in love have become a national competition. The belief that 'I have to be extraordinary' leads to striving, perfectionism, and the endless desire to prove ourselves.

The Bible is full of examples of people whose lives were marked by striving and effort. In the book of Exodus, we read that Moses sat as judge for the people, who stood around from morning to night waiting for him to adjudicate their cases. He was going it alone, and he was exhausted. It took a visit from his father-in-law Jethro to help him see the folly of his ways: 'What you are doing is not good. You and these people … will only wear yourselves out. The work is too heavy for you; you cannot handle it alone' (Exodus 18:17–18). He challenged Moses to take off his Superman cape, admit he couldn't be all things to all people, and delegate some of his responsibilities to others.

Ruth Haley Barton reflects on this story and on how, in the New Testament, Paul grapples honestly with the reality of limitations:

> When [Paul] wrote about not thinking more highly of ourselves than we ought (Romans 12:3), he was making a very general statement about limiting our grandiosity and pride by cultivating a realistic sense of our essential nature. He was talking about being willing to live *within the limits and the possibilities of who we really are*. … Living graciously within the boundaries of our life as it has been entrusted to us gives our life substance. Oddly enough, something of the will of God is contained in the very limits that

we often try to sidestep or ignore. Living within limits is not in any way an acquiescence that is despairing, passive, or fatalistic. Rather it honors the deepest realities of the life God has given us. Life in this body at this age and stage. Life in our family at its age and stage. Life in this personality. Life with this community. Life in the midst of this calling.[25]

I still have a long way to go, but I have found moments of unexpected peace and stillness on the occasions when I have learnt to live and work within the 'easy yoke' of the limits of my life.

This was a lesson learnt the hard way in the early days of working for Care for the Family. As Family Life Manager, my role included leading a gifted and capable team. Building the team in the first place came naturally to me. I found I knew instinctively how to create a compelling vision and create a sense of belonging. It was a dream job. The team gelled and now simply needed managing – how difficult could that be? I had never been given the opportunity to manage a team before and it wasn't long before I found out why. The management of projects, processes and procedures was simply not in my skill set. But, blinkered, I pressed on regardless. Every day involved striving and effort – no easy yoke in sight. It was exhausting. Relief eventually arrived in the form of an organizational restructure and the opportunity for a different role, but looking back, if I had been more able to admit my limitations, I could have caused my long-suffering team and myself much less angst. And more precious still, we may have glimpsed something of the 'easy yoke' that Jesus offers.

Another time when I experienced the discomfort of an ill-fitting yoke took place in the home. Richard and I enjoy offering hospitality, in particular sharing good food, good conversation and relaxed space around the kitchen table. But during an especially

25 Ruth Haley Barton, *Strengthening the Soul of Your Leadership: Seeking God in the Crucible of Ministry* (InterVarsity Press, 2018), pp109, 112.

busy season, I found this was taking a toll on me. I was confused. I usually love cooking and welcoming people into our home – so why was I finding it so unmanageable and utterly exhausting?

In his goodness, God sent a 'Jethro' my way with the loving challenge: 'What you are doing is not good. You will only wear yourself out.' My Jethro encouraged me to consider what hospitality meant for us within the boundaries and limits of this season of our lives. She explained that hospitality required not just physical and social energy (which I had in abundance), but also carried an emotional and spiritual cost, which for me at that time was sorely depleted. I realized that I had slipped into thinking that as a 'good Christian' I should always have an open house and had simply ploughed ahead without acknowledging the limitations of this season. Of course, hospitality means moving beyond 'nice supper parties for people like us' to having generous and open hearts and to welcoming the stranger. But on this occasion, laying down the striving and recognizing the finiteness of what I can do brought me a freedom I hadn't previously known.

Striving perfectionism is not the way of Jesus. The need to prove ourselves is a trap. It will prevent us from discovering a place of attentive stillness that will take us deeper into the transforming presence of God. It is the antithesis of the way Jesus lived.

Bookending the accounts of Jesus' ministry are two stories that bear witness to the fact that here was a man who had nothing to prove. Right at the beginning of his ministry, Jesus goes to John to be baptized. The Bible tells us that heaven was opened, the Spirit of God descended like a dove and alighted on him, and a voice from heaven proclaimed: 'This is my Son, whom I love; with him I am well pleased' (Matthew 3:17). Jesus hadn't yet told a parable or performed a single miracle – and the Father was pleased with him.

Straight away, Jesus is led by the Spirit into the desert to be tempted by the devil. Satan opens by playing what he believes is a trump card; he calls into question Jesus' very identity: '*If* you are the

Son of God …' (Matthew 4:3, my emphasis). But it is this identity that has just been affirmed by Jesus' Father, and, secure in it, Jesus stands firm.

Fast forward just three years and the apostle John invites us to accompany Jesus during the last week of his life. It was just before the Passover Feast, and the evening meal was being served. John writes:

> *Jesus knew that the Father had put all things under his power, and that he had come from God and was returning to God; so he got up from the meal, took off his outer clothing, and wrapped a towel round his waist. After that, he poured water into a basin and began to wash his disciples' feet, drying them with the towel that was wrapped round him.*
>
> JOHN 13:3–5

In his life on earth, Jesus lived *from* and not *for* the Father's approval. He was totally secure in his identity. There was no striving. He had nothing to prove.

In his bestselling book *The Boy, The Mole, The Fox and The Horse*, Charlie Mackesy uses a simple story and a series of beautiful ink drawings to convey deep truths about the human heart. One of my favourites is his picture of the boy sitting close to the fox with the mole and the horse nearby:

> 'What's your best discovery?' asked the mole.
> 'That I'm enough as I am,' the boy replies.[26]

It is only when we know deep down that we are enough, that we can make the most of opportunities that come our way, and give our best without wearing ourselves out in the process. As we begin to lay down our striving and relinquish the need to prove our worth, we will create space for God to remind us of his unconditional love for us. Our identity is secure in him.

26 Charlie Mackesy, *The Boy, the Mole, the Fox and the Horse* (Ebury Press, 2019).

The first step I needed to take as I sought to learn about the attentive stillness of the lioness was to pause, recalibrate, and remind myself that there is nothing I can do to make God love me more and nothing I can do to make him love me less.[27] We are loved for who we are. We have nothing to prove.

PAUSE TO CONSIDER:

- *What makes it difficult for you to cease striving and be still?*

- *How would you answer the question: 'What is your best discovery?'*

---

27 see Philip Yancey, *What's So Amazing About Grace?* (Harper Collins, 1997), p70.

CHAPTER 6

MOVING AT THE RIGHT SPEED

Once a lioness locates her prime position, she drops … Her presence ripples through the plain, and those closest panic and scatter. The frightened animals turn to see if the lioness has given chase. But the lioness hasn't moved. It's not time. She is still and almost imperceptible in the golden grass. She may nap as she waits but her sleep isn't deep. She's just gathering strength as she waits for the right moment to make a move.[28]

Living from a need to prove ourselves can drive us to overcommit and live our lives in a persistent state of busyness. Even if we believe in our ability to fly at speed through our days, it might perhaps be wise for us to take a moment to consider the impact on those around us. It is they who often pay the real cost.

We will examine in a later chapter how the age of digital technology has accelerated this fast-paced way of living. But other icons of our frenetic culture have also had an impact. Fast food, coffee to go, Netflix, and Amazon Prime all help us to 'take the waiting out of wanting' and create a virtue out of doing as much as we can in as little time as possible.

As I continued to discover more about what lay behind my ant-like behaviour, I realized that I had to face up to an uncomfortable truth: while busyness may give me a sense of purpose and significance, it can also chip away at the things that are most important in life.

Of course, busyness is not the basic problem. The writer of Proverbs commends the ant for her industry, and goes on to leave

28 Lisa Bevere, *Lioness Arising: Wake Up and Change Your World* (Waterbrook Press, 2011), p132.

us with the dazzling description of 'The Wife of Noble Character' (Proverbs 31:10–31). A domestic diva, she runs a small start-up, is financially savvy, manages a property portfolio, and is kind and generous – a model of good character, family life and industry. This woman is busy by any standard.

Being busy is an outward condition. It occurs when we have many things to do and is an inevitable part of life. When we are fulfilled and fully occupied with things that matter, it is healthy. And an intense spell of busyness for a short period of time – when a project deadline is looming, the week before we go on holiday (always a productive time for me!), planning a celebration, studying for an exam – is also OK. But the problem comes when long hours, overfilled diaries with no margin, or permanent stress from overstretching simply become a toxic habit – a way of life. Instead of being an outward condition, busyness is internalized, and we take on 'busy' as our identity. We then approach everything in our lives – even the quiet moments – in a hurried way.

This truth was brought home to me a few years ago. Tired of the overwhelming pace of my life, I had signed up for a course on rhythms of work and rest. I was looking forward to the first session, hoping for some practical help and insights, and set off in good time. The first lesson took place before I even stepped across the threshold.

I parked outside, grabbed my bag, slammed the car door shut and ran up the path to the front door. Kerry, who was leading the course, had heard me coming and opened the door with a quizzical look on her face. 'There's no rush,' she said. 'We have plenty of time.' And we did – there was no need for me to have run. I could have parked, taken a few deep breaths, gathered my thoughts, picked up my bag, closed the car door quietly, walked calmly down the path, and arrived in a much less frazzled state. That moment was a mirror to my life. Busyness had jumped from my diary into my soul.

An international study has demonstrated the speed at which pedestrians walk to be a reliable measure of the pace of life in a city, and it suggests that in cities around the world, this has steadily increased.

Pace around the world is 10% faster than ever before ... As people speed up in their lives they are not eating properly, exercising or seeing friends and family ... People who walk fast are also more likely to speak and eat quickly, wear a watch and get impatient ... They don't like to sit still, sit in traffic or wait in queues ... We're just moving faster and faster and getting back to people as quickly as we can – and that's minutes and not hours. That's driving us to think everything has to happen now.[29]

And this fast-paced life can be contagious. It's interesting to note when walking with a friend how unconsciously you synchronize your steps; if they are walking faster, you speed up to walk at the same pace.

Today, a flow of Uber drivers, Deliveroo riders, buses and cyclists stream across the pretty Albert Bridge that straddles the River Thames in London, but at each end there is an old sign that reminds us of a bygone era: 'All troops must break step when marching over this bridge.' When soldiers from the nearby Chelsea Barracks would march across it in step, the fear was that vibrations would reverberate and cause the bridge to sway. And when the swaying reached a peak, it would be in danger of collapse.

And the risk of accelerating to match the pace of others is also true when we are at the wheel of a car. A particular section of road on my office commute often takes drivers unawares. Over a relatively short distance, the speed limit goes from 50 to 40 mph to 30 mph and back to 40 mph again. Even though I know the

29 'What walking speeds say about us', *BBC News*, 2 May 2007, news.bbc.co.uk (accessed 10 March 2023).

restrictions, I've found it the easiest thing in the world to slip into driving at the same speed as my fellow commuters. One day, as a direct consequence of my lack of concentration, an ominous brown envelope landed on our doormat inviting me to attend a Speed Awareness Course. Those three hours of tuition turned out to be time well spent. As well as the obvious plus of avoiding points on my licence, I can also now recognize a dual carriageway (not, as I had previously believed, a road with two lanes on each side), and I learnt some fascinating facts about speed. If we are late for work, I imagine most of us would press the accelerator to make up for lost time. We believe that a little extra speed means we'll get there quicker. That is true – to a certain extent. If we drive at 70 mph it takes us 51 seconds to travel a mile. Increase our speed by 10 mph to 80 mph, and we cover a mile in 45 seconds. So to make up for a 10-minute delay, we would need to drive at 80mph for 100 miles, just in order to arrive on time.

While I was still getting my head around those calculations, the instructor showed us some graphic images illustrating the impact of speed on accident victims. He gave some tips for avoiding falling in with the speed of the moving traffic, and then landed with this nugget of wisdom: 'Driving faster makes little difference to when you arrive, but a big difference to when you can stop.' It was wisdom, I reflected, not just for drivers but for everyone as they journey through life.

Deadlines – or more specifically, writing deadlines – are a large feature of my working life; blogs, books and scripts all need to be prepared well ahead of time. In the early days, even though I had the deadline in my diary, I ended up submitting the copy with seconds to spare. I seemed unable to work at a more leisurely pace, and instead of completing a manuscript with plenty of time for it to be reviewed or finishing a talk in time for the accompanying PowerPoints and video clips to be assembled, I would fly by the seat of my proverbial pants. Thankfully, I have made progress in this area, but even now if I set aside a day for writing, before turning on my laptop I can find myself unloading the dishwasher, folding the washing, tidying my desk, checking my emails, or doing any one of a million other jobs that could quite easily wait for the evening. The truth is, living in a hurry can become a way of life. We learn to love the adrenaline kick and the feeling of being under pressure.

But living life in a state of persistent hurry is far from ideal and robs us of the capacity to cultivate the quality of attentive stillness.

A friend who delivered workplace training to business leaders often began the sessions by asking them a simple question: 'How many of you do your best work under pressure?' Without fail, these captains of industry obliged with a sea of raised hands.

But take a moment to examine the logic. Imagine that Michelangelo is putting the finishing touches onto the ceiling of the Sistine Chapel, or that Beethoven is halfway through composing the final movement of his Fifth Symphony. At lunchtime they are told to hurry up and work faster, their masterpiece needs to be done and dusted by 5pm that afternoon. The nonsense of this scenario reveals our wrong thinking. It was C.S. Lewis who said: 'I don't believe that good work is ever done in a hurry.'[30] While many of us might need an incentive to get started, the truth is, we seldom do our best work when we rush it. Our best work is done when we have time to do it properly.

And what is true for work and creativity is also true for our relationships. Hurry causes me to be distracted – so preoccupied with myself and my life that I am unable to be fully present with others, with myself, and even with God. But friendships take time, love takes time, and our relationship with God takes time.

Hurry and love are poor bedfellows. In *The Ruthless Elimination of Hurry* John Mark Comer writes:

30 C.S. Lewis, *They Stand Together: The Letters of C.S. Lewis to Arthur Greeves (1914–1963)* (Collins, 1979), p120.

All my worst moments as a father, a husband, and a pastor, even as a human being, are when I'm in a hurry – late for an appointment, behind on my unrealistic to-do list, trying to cram too much into my day. I ooze anger, tension, a critical nagging – the antitheses of love … Hurry and love are oil and water: they simply do not mix.[31]

Festive jumpers, fairy lights, and familiar carols always make Care for the Family's Christmas celebrations special. On one of these occasions after our carol service, I found myself chatting to a colleague I hadn't seen for a while. I asked how he was doing, and he began to tell me about the highs and lows of his life over the last year. I fully intended to listen, but before I knew it my mind had wandered to all the things I had to get done in this season of goodwill and, in particular, the pressing issue of what to serve alongside the traditional pudding on Christmas Day. I considered the options. *Tiramisu or chocolate torte? And caramelized oranges to go alongside? And would my sister bring whatever it was I decided on? If so, which would be easier to transport? …*

An offer of a mince pie jolted me back to reality, along with the stark realisation that I had absolutely no idea what my colleague had been saying. He'd begun our conversation by rehearsing the pros and cons of a possible house move, but my mind's diversion to Christmas Day fare meant that as we said goodbye, I had no idea what the outcome was. It was author John Ortberg who said: 'Hurry is not just a disordered schedule. Hurry is a disordered heart,'[32] and in that moment, I realized that my disordered heart had taken me on a detour. The tiramisu *vs* torte debate had trumped giving my colleague the simple gift of focused time and attention.

31 John Mark Comer, *The Ruthless Elimination of Hurry: How to stay emotionally healthy and spiritually alive in the chaos of the modern world* (Hodder & Stoughton, 2019), p23.
32 John Ortberg, *The Life You've Always Wanted: Spiritual Disciplines for Ordinary People* (Zondervan, 2009), p79.

In God's kindness, a staff gathering a few weeks later gave me a second chance, and I made a beeline for my colleague, determined to put my wandering thoughts to one side, to pause, and to be present to the moment. I have no idea if he noticed the difference, but the effect on me was palpable. Instead of drifting to my own agenda, I stayed with his. Instead of sneaking a look at my watch, and making my excuses, I felt energized and engaged. And in a way that is hard to describe, I felt the smile of God over our conversation.

By any standard, Jesus was busy, but, although his life was full, it was never hurried. He seemed in no rush to get to Jairus' house or even to be with his sick friend Lazarus. The Bible tells us that he did 'only what he [saw] his Father doing' (John 5:19). He knew the power of having a rhythm and pace of life that allowed him to give people his attention in the moment. He lived in connection with his Father and was present to whatever was going on in front of him; he lived his life from a place of rest. And he calls us to do the same.

In William Gibson's novel *Pattern Recognition*, the protagonist, Cayce, suffers badly with the disorientating, debilitating and out-of-place feeling of jet lag, something she describes as 'soul-delay'. She realizes that:

> Her mortal soul is leagues behind her, being reeled in on some ghostly umbilical down the vanished wake of the plane that brought her here ... Souls can't move that quickly, and are left behind, and must be awaited, upon arrival, like lost luggage.[33]

And there are times in our lives when we need to recognize that we have travelled too far, too fast; we need to stop and wait for our souls to catch up.

In a world dominated by speed, productivity and technology, we would do well to slow down. We may need to look beneath the

---

33 William Gibson, *Pattern Recognition* (Penguin Press, 2011), p1.

surface, chase the symptoms down to the root, and confront the inner dynamics that keep us in this way of life.

In his book *Three Mile an Hour God*, the Japanese theologian Kosuke Koyama writes:

> God walks 'slowly' because he is love. If he is not love he would have gone much faster. Love has its speed. It is an inner speed. It is a spiritual speed. It is a different kind of speed from the technological speed to which we are accustomed. It is 'slow' yet it is lord over all other speeds since it is the speed of love.[34]

If I really intend to do something about my ant-like propensity to live life in a hurry, one of the first things I need to do is to detox from the adrenaline rush of living in the fast lane – to slow down my body in order to slow down my mind, inhabit the moment, and be present to others, to myself and to God.

In 1986 a McDonald's was set up next to the celebrated Spanish Steps in Rome. The Golden Arches were seen as the antithesis of Italian food culture, and resulted in a protest which led to the Slow Food movement. In a world dominated by speed, efficiency, productivity and technology, this subversive movement advocated a culture of slowness. It soon sparked off other expressions including Slow Cinema, Slow Cities, Slow Parenting, and Slow Gardening.

While I am curious as to how gardening could be anything other than slow (and I would lay a bet that any advocate of Slow Parenting may not have had to get four children out of the house for a dentist appointment), there is wisdom to be found in the idea of applying the brake on our fast-paced lives. But the very term 'slowing down' needs interrogating to discover exactly what it means.

Instagram accounts displaying images of beautiful, unstressed, unhurried people wafting through fields of lavender in flowing linen, or sitting around firepits in chunky knit cardigans warming

---

34 Kosuke Koyama, *Three Mile an Hour God* (Orbis, 1980), p7.

their hands on large mugs of chai tea, give an attractive picture of the slow life. But in reality, it's not one that many of us can attain. Those with young children, or who, like me, are unable to clean their teeth without dribbling toothpaste on their top, wouldn't stay 'wafty' and serene in neutral linen for long. And even well-intentioned advice to bring 'slow' into the workplace by taking time out to light a scented candle during the lunch hour may cause the opposite of 'slow' with an unscheduled fire drill.

Vicky, a mother to three boys, who tried to embrace slow living, said this:

> 'As a family we were living at such a pace, and when I read about the slow movement, I decided to give it a go … Complete disaster!
>
> 'By the time I'd got up early to practise gratitude, fed my sourdough culture, replaced my coffee on-the-run in favour of a slow family breakfast, walked slowly to work, turned a blind eye to my overflowing inbox in order to read poetry in my lunch break, cooked slow food for tea (not a fish finger or baked bean in sight), stressed about finding something meaningful to scribble in my journal, then run a deep bath with essential oils at just the right temperature to ensure a good night's sleep – all ready to repeat tomorrow – I was shattered! This kind of slow might be good for some, but it wasn't for me.'

Of course, there is something to commend in each of those different exercises, but in the enthusiasm to embrace the slower life, it is easy to miss the point. Slowing down isn't simply a blanket set of practices that you lay over every aspect of your day. Rather than embracing 'slow' lock, stock and barrel, the secret is to take a step back and look at what slowing down might mean for *you* with your individual temperament, lifestyle and circumstances. For you, does slowing down mean doing less? Doing different things? Doing things differently? Simply doing the same things more slowly? Or all of the above?

And perhaps most importantly, particularly for those of us, like me, who have a natural bent for living at speed (in fact, we enjoy the thrill of it), what's the point of slowing down in the first place?

Author Carl Honoré writes:

> … the Slow philosophy is not about doing everything at a snail's pace. … [it] can be summed up in a single word: balance. … Be fast when it makes sense to be fast, and be slow when slowness is called for. Seek to live at what musicians call the *tempo giusto* – the right speed.[35]

Tempo giusto resonates with me. I have struggled over the years with the term 'work-life balance'. There is often a tension between what our souls need and what is expected of us. Life can be unpredictable. There are crises at work and crises at home, sometimes one after the other, sometimes all at once – and my experience is that it's virtually impossible to keep life 'in balance'. When there's a project deadline, staffing shortage, or important client event to be organized, the workplace requires our energy and focus. And conversely when there's illness, teenage angst, exam pressure, or a leaking roof, it's all hands to the pump in the home. Sometimes in life we can't avoid the need to accelerate our efforts and live 'fast'. The problem is that once the crisis is over, we don't remember to take our foot off the pedal and slow down.

My friend conducted an experiment with living slow and I arranged to meet up with him to find out what he had discovered. Frustratingly, I was unable to find anywhere to park and when I finally found a space, I couldn't activate the app in order to pay. When I eventually got it to work, I sprinted down the road to the

---

35 Carl Honoré, *In Praise of Slow: How a Worldwide Movement is Challenging the Cult of Speed* (Orion, 2005), p15.

café where we'd agreed to meet. Panting and gasping to catch my breath, I apologized for being late. The irony wasn't lost on either of us!

Recovering my equilibrium over a welcome cup of coffee, I was able to listen as my friend described how rather than continuing with his self-imposed hectic agenda, he had decided to try allowing the day to develop at its own pace. In particular, he started to do things more slowly than usual – washing, eating, talking, walking. He would deliberately make choices that involved waiting – arriving early for appointments, joining the longest queue at the checkout, and driving in the slowest lane in traffic. This simple exercise, he reflected, had helped him focus on the present, and as he did so, he discovered unexpected moments when he encountered the presence of God. I reflected that whatever the circumstances, there is something we can all learn from his experience.

For some of us, doing things slowly may not be the answer. It may mean doing less or doing things differently. My children are now adults, but I learnt this lesson when they were five, seven, nine and eleven years old. Keen for them to be proficient in the water, I made enquiries about swimming lessons. Other parents at school recommended an excellent teacher, Kim, who ran classes on a Monday after school. The only drawback was that it was at a pool on the far side of the city. Even more inconvenient was the fact that, because of their range of age and ability, the lessons for my children didn't take place at the same time. This meant that every Monday we had to dash straight from school in order to set up camp in the hot, steamy, chlorine-filled atmosphere of the pool for several hours. It certainly didn't make for the most restful start to the week! However, I was determined that they should learn to swim and this seemed the only way to make it happen. Head down and blinkered, I pressed on.

Before long, the children were asking to do other after-school activities that 'everyone else' was doing: Brownies, Cubs, judo, recorder, football, tennis and – the straw that broke the camel's back – gymnastics. Each of the activities required a trip in the car to deliver and collect the child/children and extra friends, often in rush-hour traffic, and soon every day of the week was taken up with an activity. Without us making a conscious decision, we had drifted into living at a hurried, unsustainable pace.

That summer at a conference, I attended a talk called 'Rhythms of Life'. (It seems the Holy Spirit was challenging my ant-like behaviour even then!) The speaker talked about the tyranny of busyness and a frantic pace of life that not only takes its toll on us and those we love, but means that we leave no space in our day for the possibility of encountering the presence of God. As he spoke, my mind reflected on the Monday swimming marathon and other after-school activities that came a close second, and I resolved to make some changes. We are fortunate to live near the centre of our community and on our return, I decided to limit after-school activities to those we could walk to. Any activity that involved loading four children in to the car, driving across the city through rush-hour traffic, and then doing the whole procedure in reverse would stop. That simple decision didn't give me 'Mother of the Year' award, but it changed our lives. We found a swimming teacher at the local school and although she may not have been as experienced or qualified as the excellent Kim, she did the job we wanted. While our children will never be in the GB swimming squad, they did all get badges on their towels as proof that they could stay afloat. And in the bargain, we learnt an important lesson about staying afloat in the cultural ocean of a too-busy life.

We all have different responsibilities and pressures, so the important thing is to find a rhythm that works for us in the season of life we're in. My nephew *did* go on to be in the GB gymnastics team. So for his parents, mad drives not just across the city but across the country, were something they had to learn to navigate –

both literally and metaphorically – by making adjustments in the rest of life.

During a very pressurized and busy season in the workplace, when Richard felt that the speed of life was relentless, he made some courageous decisions in order to make space and slow down. He stood down from a number of boards and resigned from some voluntary positions, laying down good things that he'd enjoyed doing. As difficult as it was to make those decisions, it's something that he doesn't regret. An unsustainable, hurried lifestyle can creep up on us unawares. Take a stock check and ask yourself how your diary impacts your ability to live in the present and make room for God. And then, if necessary, take drastic action to change things.

When I first shared my desire to live at a slower pace, a friend who knows me well laughed at the very suggestion. He said: 'You thrive off being busy; you won't ever slow down.' My desire to be more like the lioness caused me to feel irritated at his comment, and I became defensive, arguing that it was more about pace on the inside than the outside. It was quite possible to live at a measured pace on the inside while having a full, busy (and, I confess, often hurried) lifestyle. He told me that was a cop-out. We agreed to differ.

On reflection, however, I acknowledged that there was a kernel of truth in what he was saying. I thought of the lioness, peaceful and still in the shade of the tree, her cubs around her, but all her senses on high alert, ready to respond in the moment.

There will be times when we keep our foot on the accelerator. But there are also times when we need to slow down and be still. We don't always have to make drastic changes – small adjustments can also make a difference, but when we do make time to slow down our bodies, we will find our minds have space to focus on the present. And it is then that we will make room for the presence and the activity of God in our lives.

PAUSE TO CONSIDER:

- *What is the cost to you, and to those you live and work with, of living in a persistent state of busyness?*

- *What difference would it make if you could live from a soul that is at rest?*

- *What does slowing down mean for you? Doing less? Doing different things? Doing the same things differently? All of these or something else?*

- *What one small change could you make today to slow down?*

CHAPTER 7

SEEING IN THE DARK

[Elsa], of course, could not know why we were doing such a senseless thing as to struggle across sharp lava at night, and it was only her affection for us and her trust that kept her going. In spite of the hardships she had endured on this safari, in the course of which she had walked well over 300 miles, the bond between us had only been strengthened. As long as she was with us and knew herself to be loved and secure, she was happy.[36]

A knock at the door, a text message, an early morning phone call, an email or a letter – for each of us there may come a moment when something crashes into our life, ushering in anxiety and fear, and robbing us of our peace.

I was about to go on stage to speak at a Care for the Family event when I got the text. I was in the green room, going over my notes, and making the most of the Mint Imperials that our hosts had kindly left out for us. As I switched my phone to airplane mode, I noticed it. Breaking my rule never to be distracted by reading a message just before speaking, I clicked 'open'. It was from one of our children who was working at the Houses of Parliament at that time. He appeared to have sent me a picture of his feet from an odd vantage point under a desk. The room seemed unusually dark. Curious, I scrolled down:

> 'Hi Mum. Terrorists in the building. Please pray. Will keep you posted. PS love you.'

In that minute, it was as if all the air was sucked from my lungs, my head started spinning and I felt sick. It was 7.26pm and in just four minutes

36 Joy Adamson, *Born Free* (Pantheon Books, 1960), p64.

I needed to make my way to the stage. Praying harder than I have ever prayed before, I took a deep breath and entered the auditorium. Trying to focus on the job in hand, I did my level best over the next hour to deliver marriage advice to the good people of Sheffield.

The events were being reported in real time on BBC News, but it wasn't until later that evening that Richard and I were finally able to make contact with our son. He was working for a senior politician whose office was directly under Big Ben, and late that afternoon he'd been called into the office to help with some paperwork. As he sorted through the papers, he heard a commotion outside the window. Right before his eyes, a man wielding two long knives was attacking a policeman who fell to the ground. The sound of gunfire opened all around. It was the day of the terrorist activity on Westminster Bridge.

We heard later that a man had driven an SUV into pedestrians on the bridge, got out of the car and run onto the Parliamentary Estate, fatally stabbing PC Keith Palmer. He then ran towards the MPs' entrance looking for more victims. In the commotion, no one at the scene had any idea what was happening. It turned out that the gunfire was from the security services, but in the mayhem, my son and his colleagues thought there might be more people involved who would storm Parliament, their machine guns raining bullets everywhere. Putting the well-rehearsed drill into action, they took the name off their office door, piled furniture against it, turned off the lights, lay under the desk and waited.

I have received hundreds of text messages from that child over the years. Messages asking me to deliver forgotten football boots (answer generally 'no') or a forgotten inhaler (answer 'yes'), giving me news of exam results, or letting me know he'd missed the bus home. But the text he sent that evening was different. I realized there was every chance it might be the last one I received.

How do our hearts respond in moments like that? When, in a second, life changes. When it looks like we are going to a place we don't want to be?

On that occasion, the crisis was relatively short, but in my work at Care for the Family, we support many families whose worst fears have been realized – there has been no happy ending.

I think of the mother whose teenage son has been sentenced to serve time in a youth detention centre, the young couple whose longed-for child was born with severe disabilities, the wife who discovers her husband's porn addiction, or the man who stumbles upon his wife's affair, as well as many other heartbreaking stories of loss and bereavement.

Perhaps you will have had this experience too, but it feels as if I have been to too many funerals of people who have died before their time. In particular, I think of my brother-in-law who died much too young, leaving behind my sister and her two children. As I got up to speak during the service, I looked at the children sitting in the front row and railed against this injustice. Death is an intruder, an enemy.

Through my work, I have the privilege of spending time with parents who have lost a child or with those who have been widowed young. Listening to them and their families describe their grief journey has been like walking on holy ground. They and countless others have helped me accept that there are no concise, easy answers to the problem of suffering in our hurting, broken world; no neat framework to contain it.

We often think about life's journey as being one of hills and valleys – moments of joy followed by times of difficulty and back again. But pastor Rick Warren has an alternative view. He talks about life being on parallel tracks – the twin tracks of battles and blessings.

On the track of blessing, life is good. Friends and family relationships are thriving; if we are parents, our children are doing well; and if we are in ministry, we are seeing times of fruitfulness and growth. But running alongside that track of blessing is the track of battles – the track where bad, often unexpected, things happen: failed relationships, children breaking our hearts, health challenges, redundancy, conflict in the workplace, financial pressure. Sometimes we see these things coming, but so often they come from nowhere.

Times of joy and celebration run right alongside times of grief, disappointment and despair. And we will each have our share of both. When an unexpected crisis crashes in on our lives, it's understandable that it knocks us sideways. We can feel overwhelmed with fear, grief and anxiety, and it is natural to experience those emotions. There are times when we are just hanging on, relying on the support and prayers of others.

I have seen enough heartache in families I've worked with over the years to know that tragedy is no respecter of persons. While some seem to have more than their fair share of sadness and despair, all of us at some time or other will encounter times of challenge, disappointment or regret. As well as family tragedy, it might be the gut-wrenching feeling of disillusionment as we watch the glittering promotion we had been promised handed to another, or the sense of betrayal when a trusted colleague uses our database to set up a rival company of their own. It could be that we've trained for years for the competition of a lifetime, only to have to pull out because of injury in the preliminary rounds, or that we witness the start-up we invested our life savings in crumble around us. Perhaps we simply feel without direction in a sea of confusion for months on end, or we look the ticking clock in the eye and realize that the dreams and ambitions we had as a twenty-something have slipped from our grasp.

As challenges and disappointments come our way, irritations and frustrations cast a shadow over our day, or tragedies occur that change the course of our lives. How can we learn to live so that they don't crush us? How do we deal with them in such a way that we are not continually caught up in regrets of what might have been or fear of what could be? How, to quote Kipling, can we 'meet with Triumph and Disaster, and treat those two imposters just the same'?[37] How, like the lioness, can we remain in that place of quiet strength?

In the summer of 1940, 350,000 Allied soldiers found themselves trapped on the beaches of Normandy. The German army were advancing and gaining ground; the situation was desperate. In the midst of this crisis, when all looked lost, an officer from the British Navy is reported to have sent an urgent message back to London. It contained just three words: 'But if not ...'

The meaning of those words might well be lost on many today, but Prime Minister Winston Churchill understood. He recognized that they were from the book of Daniel, and that they'd been spoken by three courageous young men who had found themselves in an equally desperate situation, with little hope of escape. Shadrach, Meshach and Abednego had been taken into captivity to Babylon in the seventh century BC as part of the Jewish exile and had entered the service of King Nebuchadnezzar. As worshippers of the one true God, Yahweh, they had refused to obey the King's edict to bow down to his golden statue. Furious at their disobedience, the King decreed that, unless they knelt before it, they would be thrown into a blazing furnace.

The Bible records their courageous response:

Shadrach, Meshach and Abednego answered and said to the king, 'O Nebuchadnezzar, we have no need to answer you in this matter. If this be so, our God whom we serve is able to deliver us from the burning fiery furnace, and he will deliver us out of your hand, O king. But if not, be it known to you, O king, that we will not serve your gods or worship the golden image that you have set up.'

DANIEL 3:16–18 (ESV)

---

37 Rudyard Kipling, 'If' in *'If' And Other Poems* (Michael O'Mara Books, 2002, 2016) pp73-74.

When we feel as if our backs are against the wall, when life throws us a curveball, it is understandable that we want all to be well. But I find the 'But if not' of those three young men so remarkable because, in essence, it said, 'Even if our prayers go unanswered, even if our worst fears come true, that will not be the last word. You may take our lives, but because of our faith in God, that will not be the end of the story. And that causes us to cry out even in the midst of our trauma: "We will still trust Him."'

This is a cry for the darkest of times, a reaching out for hope in the middle of the fiercest storm. The most profound example of this that I can think of occurred on the last night of Jesus' life. He is in the garden of Gethsemane – the name itself has come to epitomise the very hardest times of our lives – and he cries out to God, 'Let this cup pass from me.'

> *He withdrew about a stone's throw beyond them, knelt down and prayed, 'Father, if you are willing, take this cup from me; yet not my will, but yours be done.*
>
> LUKE 22:41-42

He is speaking of the cup of incredible suffering – both physical and spiritual – that awaits him the next day as, nailed to a cross, he bears the sin of the world. But at the end of his prayer he adds, 'Yet not my will, but yours be done.' This is Jesus' 'But if not.' It is a declaration that even in our darkest night, our lives are in the hand of God. Everyone who has not had their prayer answered in the way they wanted can read of this moment in Gethsemane and know they are not alone.

We can only guess what thoughts raced through the mind of that young British officer as he faced what seemed like inevitable annihilation on the beaches of northern France, that summer day in 1940. But somehow those three words, the very same words spoken by three young men in ancient Babylon, came rolling down the years to bring a message not just of comfort, but of strength.

To Winston Churchill, the message was clear: the Allied forces were in great danger, and yet they were trusting God for a miracle. But even if there wasn't one, they weren't going to give in.

Hindsight is a great thing; we know that the Bible story ends well. The three friends were saved from the fiery furnace. And what Churchill called 'a miracle of deliverance' took place at Dunkirk. The weather changed, the Luftwaffe were grounded, and the British people sprang into action, setting out across the Channel with shipping vessels, pleasure cruisers and small fishing boats to bring more than 338,000 soldiers to safety. But when Shadrach, Meshach and Abednego said those words 'But if not ...', they didn't know the end of the story.

When life doesn't turn out as we hoped, when we suffer disappointment, heartache and loss, when we are in the midst of the most difficult circumstances with no knowledge of how things will turn out, can we say those words too? 'I know my God can deliver me. But even if he does not, I will trust him anyway'?

Pete Greig writes about Holy Saturday, the day between Good Friday and Easter Sunday:

> ... although we know so little about it, Holy Saturday seems to me to describe the place in which many of us live much of our lives: waiting for God to say something, or do something or make sense of the things we are experiencing.[38]

In his book *God on Mute*, Pete expands on this:

> We know that Jesus died for us yesterday. We trust that there may be miracles tomorrow. But what of today – this eternal Sabbath when heaven is silent? Where, we wonder, is God now?[39]

---

38 Pete Greig, 'Where is God when heaven is silent?', *PETEGREIG.INFO*, April 20, 2019, dirtyglory.org (accessed 13 March 2023).
39 Pete Greig, *God on Mute: Engaging the Silence of Unanswered Prayer* (David C. Cook, 2007), p237.

There are times in our lives when we find ourselves waiting on the Dunkirk beach or looking into the fiery furnace like Daniel's friends. It is Easter Saturday and often the temptation is to fast forward, to want certainty and sanitized answers. But maybe we shouldn't rush too quickly to Easter Sunday. Like the first disciples, we may need to live for a while in the uncomfortable place of not knowing how things are going to turn out. It is when we are sad, scared, confused and even doubting that so often we discover God doing his deepest work in our lives.

But living in that place of uncertainty is hard. Experts tell us that early experiences of family, and particularly of father figures, influence how we see God. My own father was a kind, gentle and generous man. He died, aged 100, on Christmas Day, which was ironic as in many ways he was a bit of a Father Christmas; his main way of showing love was to give gifts. I remember that when my bike was stolen it was my father who bought a replacement. And when we moved into our first flat and the heating didn't work, it was my father who arranged a delivery of coal for the fire. His generosity influenced how I came to see God. I saw my heavenly Father as someone who gives good gifts to his daughter and steps in to make life all right.

But with the responsibility of adulthood came issues that couldn't be fixed. I found that God didn't always step in straightaway to make things right. Sometimes difficult situations didn't get sorted. I was left needing to recalibrate my life, and find out how when things didn't work out, I could live in such a way that my happiness didn't depend on my circumstances.

I have discovered, as those saints much wiser than me have over the years, that when life doesn't seem to make sense or work out as we hoped, and when prayers remain unanswered, there is a bigger gift than changed circumstances: it is the gift of God's presence.

I will never forget a conversation I had with a friend whose little girl had been diagnosed with an inoperable brain tumour. Friends rallied round, we prayed our best prayers and cried out to God, pleading for her life. But after a rollercoaster of glimmers of hope one minute followed by crashing disappointment the next, she eventually lost the battle. A few years on her mother reflected:

'I realized I had a choice. I could continue to be angry with God and allow this tragedy to overshadow my life and change what I knew of him so far. Or I could try to make peace with the fact that my prayers weren't answered, and reach out to him anyway. It wasn't easy, and it's an ongoing process, but I have tried to put the weight of this unanswered prayer on "the mystery shelf". I wanted to be able to trust my heavenly Father who until then I knew to be good, rather than putting my trust in the outcome.'

None of us will be immune from the pain and disappointment of life. Psalm 23 reminds us that 'even though [we] walk through the darkest valley', he is with us (verse 4). And in moments of challenge, time and again I have found refuge in the Psalms, particularly the Psalms of Lament. In fact, during the trauma of the Covid-19 pandemic, many churches rediscovered the beautiful art of lament – the opening our hearts to God in a raw expression of grief and sorrow. As pastor and author Tyler Staton writes:

Scripture makes it clear that God collects two things – prayers and tears … God is bottling up my tears and saving them right next to my prayers … both are key ingredients in the recipe of redemption … he loves us too much to let either go to waste.[40]

We may think that it's wrong to feel emotions like anger, frustration, confusion or sorrow – or, even worse, to express those emotions to God. But the Bible teaches the very opposite. This is not about mindless positive thinking or denying the circumstances. Instead,

40 Tyler Staton, *Praying Like Monks, Living Like Fools: An Invitation to the Wonder and Mystery of Prayer* (Hodder Faith, 2022) pp177, 184.

we can face the challenges of life head on, doing what we can, but knowing we can't make everything right and continuing to trust God anyway.

Of course, when trials come our way, we may be thrown into turmoil, but in time, can we learn to say with St Paul and others after him that we 'have learned the secret of being content in any and every situation' (Philippians 4:12)? In other words, can we learn to live so that the barometer of our peace is not our changing circumstances, but the unchanging nature of God's love and care for us and his presence with us?

Returning again to our trip to South Africa, I remember one evening, when we were on our way back from a game drive. It was late and the night was clear, a few stars giving pinpricks of light in the African sky. From the front seat, our guide was shining a small torch around, and to be honest I wondered what difference it would make – the darkness was all-encompassing. Pulling over to the side of the sandy track he shone the beam at a rocky outcrop a few hundred yards away. In that moment, two lights reflected back. It was a lioness – her body concealed in the darkness but her cat's eyes shining for us all to see. Our guide explained to us that in the pitch dark, lions are as blind as we are. But their pupils are different to ours, and their eyes are designed to help them pick up, amplify and reflect even the faintest light. If there is a glimmer of light punctuating the darkness – from the beam of a torch, or the dim light of the moon or stars – it is caught and transformed into sight.

For the lioness, it is as though the light comes from within her eyes rather than from her environment, enabling her to see things in the darkness where we would not. Can we learn to see in the dark in such a way that the light we live by comes not from the darkness of our circumstances, but from the light that lives within us?

Time and again David dwells on his experience of God's luminous presence in the most testing of times. He declares:

If I say, 'Surely the darkness will hide me
and the light become night around me,'
even the darkness will not be dark to you;
the night will shine like the day,
for darkness is as light to you.

PSALM 139:11-12

A few hundred years later the prophet Isaiah brings a similar message of hope to a people in exile:

Fear not, for I have redeemed you;
I have called you by name, you are mine.
When you pass through the waters, I will be with you;
and through the rivers, they shall not overwhelm you.
When you walk through the fire, you will not be burned,
and the flame shall not consume you.

ISAIAH 43:1-2 (ESV)

As much as we would like them to, these verses don't say we won't ever walk through the fire. But they say that when we do, God promises to be with us.

In the story of the three friends and the fiery furnace, there was one thing that didn't survive the flames. The Bible says that after the Lord rescued Shadrach, Meshach and Abednego from the furnace there was not even any smell of fire on them. The only thing that was burned were the ropes that had bound them.

The truth is that so often it is when we go through tough times that God does his deepest purifying work in our lives. He can use these times to deal with the things that bind us: attitudes, habits, limited ways of thinking – anything that holds us captive and prevents us from living freely.

The world tells us to do everything we can to avoid or escape difficult circumstances, to keep ourselves busy in ant formation, but in the Gospels, we see that time and again Jesus stops and meets people in their pain. Of course, he cares about our circumstances, and he can and does step in to change things. But ultimately, he is concerned about our heart; in challenging times he wants to bring about transformation to make us more like him, to bring us freedom.

PAUSE TO CONSIDER:

- *What battles and blessings are you experiencing at the moment?*
- *Are you waiting for God to do something or say something?*
- *Are there things in your life for which you can trust God and say 'but if not'? If so, what are they?*

CHAPTER 8

LOOKING UP

> Rocks were her favourite places, and she always chose the top of a cliff or some other safe position as her lookout.[41]

She has been my trusted companion now for a number of years. Always by my side, she is loyal and attentive, bringing me what I want at any time of the day or night, and sometimes even helping me discover things I didn't know I needed in the first place. Colourful and interesting, she is great company. It's so easy to spend time with her; in fact, the hours slip by without my realizing it. She helps me connect with old acquaintances, introduces me to new friends, and gives me a window into the highlights of their lives. Dressed for this season in fashionable grey, she reminds me of my appointments, pays for my coffee, recommends music to listen to, and even helps me keep track of my children's whereabouts. And during the Covid-19 lockdowns, her presence was a genuine lifeline. Sometimes she runs out of energy, but then I plug her in … and all is well.

The digital age has undoubtedly brought huge advantages to society, and especially so during the pandemic. Social distancing didn't have to lead to social isolation. Work meetings, school lessons, pub quiz nights, playdates, sessions at the gym, home group meetings and church services – in fact, nearly every area of our lives – moved online. This dramatic surge in the use of technology has brought about structural shifts in our online behaviour, integrating it still further into our everyday lives, and many of those changes are here to stay. But, for all the advantages, this has also come at a cost. The smartphone in our pocket causes many of us to live distracted lives and, in particular, impacts our discipleship and our walk with Jesus.

41 Joy Adamson, *Born Free* (Pantheon Books, 1960), pp69–70.

I recently went to a fascinating exhibition in London which explored the non-stop nature of twenty-first-century living in the West, and in particular, our relationship with technology. Through a range of creative exhibits, it shone a light into a world where, as the brochure said: 'we are sleeping less … complex systems exert control over us and the pull of the screen disrupts our instincts to daydream and pay attention to the world around us and each other.'[42]

One of the first things that caught my eye was the well-known work of art, *Arkwright's Cotton Mills by Night*, painted by the British artist Joseph Wright in 1782. Two large factory buildings sit uncomfortably in a peaceful rural scene. But apart from this incongruity, what is most striking is the artist's depiction of light. A full moon lights up the sky and the clouds, in marked contrast to the pinpoints of light in the many windows lit by gas lamps in the cotton mills. Artists have often portrayed changes in society, in particular how we live and work, and this painting is no exception. Artificial lighting meant that, for the first time, people could work 24-7, and in factories and mills such as this one, a human labour force including many children were working in continuous 12-hour shifts. Work had become disconnected from family and community, from the environment, and from the rhythm of day and night.

It struck me that if the artist had been commenting on society today, the windows might well be illuminated not by gas lamps but by the reflection of glowing screens. And the screens wouldn't be restricted to inside the building. Advances in digital technology now mean that we are available not just at any time of day or night, but also at any place. For perhaps the first time in history, there is nowhere to hide.

It was Herbert Simon, the 1978 Nobel Prize-winning economist, who first said that we live in an 'attention economy'.[43] In the early days of Google, former CEO Eric Schmidt famously predicted that

42 Somerset House, *A Wake-Up Call for a Non-Stop World*, edited by Sarah Cook, back cover text.
43 BER staff, 'Paying Attention: The Attention Economy', *Berkeley Economic Review*, March 31, 2020.

'the dominant global corporations would be those that succeeded in maximizing the number of 'eyeballs' they could consistently engage and control.'[44] And sure enough, the greatest commodity sought by tech giants today is no longer minerals, gold or precious metals, but our attention. The invasive ping of the notifications on our screens (generally an eye-catching shade of red) are all designed to grab our attention and interrupt our day. Art critic and historian Jonathan Crary writes that one of the goals of the tech industry is to achieve 'a relatively unbroken engagement with illuminated screens of diverse kinds that unremittingly demand interest or response.'[45] In fact, a 2016 study found that the average person touched their phone an astonishing 2,617 times per day; or had a screen time of approximately two and a half hours in a 24-hour period. Just three years later those hours had doubled.[46]

Our relationship with technology undoubtedly has an impact on our spiritual formation, so it is important that we understand the influential forces at play – in particular the power of anticipation and reward.

En route to the Grand Canyon a number of years ago, I spent a night in Las Vegas, a city known for its casinos. I can still recall the sight of people sitting in front of slot machines, locked into an addictive cycle of play. The features of anticipation and reward that keep people gambling have also been harnessed well by tech designers and explain why social media is so compelling. The reward system in our brains that drive us to check our notifications and pull the lever of a slot machine are surprisingly similar, so much so that psychologists have called it 'the slot machine effect'. Slot machines are designed to draw us into the 'zone' – that point where we become so caught up in what we are doing that we are completely unaware of what is going on around us. In Las Vegas, I noticed that there were no clocks or windows in the gambling

---

44 Jonathan Crary, *24/7: Late Capitalism and the Ends of Sleep* (Verso, 2014), p75.
45 Ibid.
46 Julia Naftulin, 'Here's how many times we touch our phones every day,' *Insider*, 13 July 2016, businessinsider.com (accessed 10 March 2023).

areas to deter people from noticing the time. They encourage constant play, give positive reinforcement, and pay out with small regular wins to keep us engaged. Social media uses exactly the same features, but instead of money, the cost is our time and attention.

The same surprise element of reward that keeps people at the roulette wheel also keeps them eyeballing their social media apps. A 'follow' or a 'like' gives the reward of social approval, which triggers a surge of dopamine in our brain – the 'feel-good hormone' that gives us a sense of pleasure and leaves us wanting more. And the very nature of 'likes' is that they are variable, and therefore more compelling. Technology companies have developed increasingly sophisticated algorithms that analyse what we search for online. After searching for an item, we are distracted by offers for similar things – wrinkle-eradicating cosmetics, magic kitchen gadgets, holidays in the sun or any other product we might have shown an interest in.

THE THIEF OF TIME

Distraction is the thief of time. She is rude; she interrupts and asks to borrow our attention. We readily lend it to her and find she invites us on a journey to new and exciting places. Sometimes it takes minutes; at other times, hours. Part of the fun is that there is no end destination and we love the ride. Occasionally, we check our watch and can't believe how time has flown! And sometimes we realize she has given us a one-way ticket and there is no easy way back. She elbows her way into our lives and squeezes out the things that matter.

I have to confess I am disappointed how often I find myself distracted by my phone. I seem to have lost the art of waiting. In the coffee queue, in the doctor's surgery, waiting for the checkout to become available, waiting for worship to begin, even when I'm queuing for the loo, a Pavlovian response causes my hand to reach for my phone. The odd thing is, there is generally no urgent need to check my messages, no important information to glean; I am simply checking Instagram, taking a look at WhatsApp messages, scrolling through posts or deleting emails. The phone has become a digital pacifier. And it feels so good.

Psychologists have coined the phrase 'technoference' to describe the phenomenon of our phones getting in the way of communication with others. We all too easily become an absent presence, physically in the room, but distracted and inattentive to others – not only to our family and friends, but to the presence of God.

At home, Richard and I try to be disciplined about not having phones by the bed, but in recent weeks one of our grandchildren was due to be born, and we were on the starting blocks to provide childcare for her sibling. Realizing that labour could start in the night, I kept my phone by the bed so we could spring into action as necessary. While that was all well and good, after the baby was born, my phone failed to make the journey of a few yards back to the charger on the landing. She remained happily by my bed. And I gave her my love and attention. It was the first thing I looked at in the morning and the last thing I looked at before I went to sleep. Instead of night-time prayers or reading a psalm, I found myself scrolling through the day's events on Twitter. It wasn't a decision I'd made – just a habit I slipped into.

Two years of transferring our lives online during lockdown has also brought about a change in our digital habits. As London School of Economics' Professor Sonia Livingstone comments:

> We've moved, I'd suggest, from seeing technology as a valued addition to our lives, to seeing technology as vital infrastructure. And as Covid-19 has made really clear, for young people especially, life is digital by default.[47]

47 Elena Martellozzo, 'Life is digital by default – so what's the impact on young people's mental health?', *London School of Economics*, 21 December 2020, blogs. lse.ac.uk (accessed 10 March 2023).

As a family we have a very lively WhatsApp group, and scrolling through the posts, quips and gifs always makes me smile. But recently, I realized I'd slipped into the habit of looking at my phone much more often, not just to check the latest WhatsApp family update, but to check emails and pop by Instagram while I am at it. I decided I would take action to break this habit and a trip with Richard to Northern Ireland for a conference seemed as though it would be a good time to go cold turkey. I turned the phone off for 24 hours. Bliss …

My euphoria was short-lived. When I turned the phone back on I was greeted with an avalanche of messages. A friend had been expecting not only to come to our house for supper but also to stay the night; however, confusion over dates had left her banging on our door in Bristol and (obviously) unable to reach us on the phone. My all-or-nothing approach wasn't perhaps the best plan, so I resolved to wean myself off the screen in a way that wouldn't massively inconvenience others. This included archiving some chats and setting up specific ringtones on others which on occasions allowed me to stay in touch with those I wanted!

Of course, it's not just our phones. While there is nothing wrong with screens per se, Amazon Prime movies, Netflix, box sets, gaming and good old-fashioned television can also steal our time. And poor boundaries around emails and work-related messages can mean that we are available 24-7. Screens are a distraction, and they can distract us in our relationship with Jesus.

Without a doubt, we are not on a level playing field. Technology means that there will always be something online that is more informative, surprising, funny, diverting or impressive than anything in our immediate, actual circumstances. The fight is on for our attention, and so we need to be intentional in putting boundaries around our use of technology.

'PARENT YOUR PHONE'

The reminder to 'parent your phone' packs a punch. In the same way that parents set the standards of behaviour in the home, including deciding when children go to bed, when they get up, where they go and when, it is vital that we control our phone rather than the phone taking charge of us. We are the parents.

A popular rainy-day activity for my children was tenpin bowling. And the secret to a peaceful afternoon (and increased opportunity for a strike!) was being able to ask for the bumpers to be raised on the alley. When the bumpers are in place, they prevent the ball from rolling off into the gutter and out of play. In the same way, we can put some 'bumpers' in place to make sure that our relationship with digital technology doesn't take us off course in our time with God.

FAMILY MEDIA AGREEMENT

When I talk to parents about managing technology in the home, one of my top tips is to draw up a 'family media agreement'. It can be done by any family, whatever its size or shape, and involves getting everyone to sit down together (including little ones and teenagers) and agree ground rules for screen use. Rules will inevitably get broken, but the important thing is that everyone has a say, and agrees to them in the first place. It's the equivalent of a digital Rule of Life (which is something we will talk more about in a later chapter) and simply sets out clear guidelines for the use of technology in the home. Whether we live alone or with others, having boundaries in place makes it much easier to keep the distraction of technology in check and create space for God (and other people).

Within this agreement, it might be helpful to consider issues such as:

How much screen time?
Bear in mind that not all screen time is the same. Endlessly scrolling through ads on social media late at night is very different to a work Zoom call, and messaging friends is different from using a phone

for devotions or using a prayer app. Most phones now offer a weekly screen time update (which can be sobering!) to help us make sure our screen use isn't creeping up unawares.

Where and when?

Are there times when and places where it would be better not to have a phone? You might consider a 'no screens at the meal table' rule. One family we know has a 'leave the phone at home' habit. If they go out for a walk or for a coffee with a friend, they sometimes make a point of leaving their phones at home. Experts say that when we're in company, perhaps at a work meeting or having a coffee with someone, the mere presence of our phone in our line of sight is a distraction and makes the person we are with less positive towards us. Perhaps that's because it feels like there is someone else present, and the truth is … there is.

Reading the Bible on a phone is obviously convenient; it's easy to follow the passage during a talk and offers a great opportunity for devotions on the bus or train. And for those of us who have trouble locating the books of Habakkuk or Jude, a digital search is much quicker than thumbing through the index. But it is all too easy to get diverted and drift into editing emails, pinning on Pinterest or snapping on Snapchat while we're en route to finding the passage. A paper Bible may be more cumbersome, but it does minimize the chance of distraction.

What about phones in the bedroom? What we look at first thing in the morning and just before we go to sleep can shape our day, so deciding to ban them from the bedroom might be something to prioritize. A multi-charger that takes care of all the family's phones outside the bedroom at night is a great idea. And when a friend's son argued that he needed his phone by his bed to wake him up in the morning, I had an easy tip to give him. Buy an alarm clock!

One way to avoid being distracted is to prevent the interruptions happening in the first place. Some things to try include:

- Turning off notifications.
- Moving the most enticing apps off the screen.
- Turning the phone to greyscale – it seems so boring!
- Loosening any love affair with emails and taking them off the phone.
- Keeping the phone out of sight during devotions. As Superman found with kryptonite, the farther away the better.

These tips just scratch the surface, but anything we can do to put boundaries around our romance with gadgets and look up from our screens is going to help us free up space for time with God and others.

It's not all negative. In fact, there's much to celebrate about the ways in which technology can help direct us into God's presence. Here are some ideas:

- *Keeping in touch* – Our small group WhatsApp chat is one of the liveliest on my phone. It's a place where we can share needs and celebrate answers to prayer.
- *Giving reminders* – Set an alarm on your phone to remind you to pray or direct your thoughts to God – it might be to pray the Lord's Prayer at lunchtime or to read a psalm before an important meeting.
- *Staying informed* – Choose to listen to good podcasts or online devotions.
- *Double listening* – Author and theologian John Stott used to advocate the practise of 'double listening' – speaking and preaching with 'the Bible in one hand and the newspaper in the other'. Can we practise 'double listening' by finding a reliable online news source to inform our prayers?
- *Listening to music* – Create playlists of different types of music that can draw you into God's presence and cause your hearts to respond in confession, thanksgiving or praise.
- *Building connections* – Find trustworthy social media accounts to follow, and respond to messages in a life-giving way.

- *Sending encouragements* – I am not generally a lists person, but I do have a little book where I write the names of people I want to pray for during the month. And I've found that having a phone with me helps me to 'put flesh' on my prayers. As I see a name on the list, I sometimes send a word of encouragement or a message to let them know I am thinking of them. Having the phone next to me means I do it in the moment – if I left it until later in the day I would probably forget!

Some time after speaking about the issue of screen use at a conference, I was so encouraged to receive this email from a young mother:

'I've realised that my bad phone habit has become an addiction and has been really affecting me, not leaving me with any time to do things that bring me peace or time to connect with others.

Following your talk, I took some steps on Friday. I deleted Instagram and Facebook, changed phone to greyscale, and deleted all apps apart from the basics. At night, I have moved the phone to charge downstairs, but I also leave it out of reach for most of the evening. I feel really different since doing this. I think it was controlling me so much. I now feel like I've taken back control and am making healthier decisions about my use of time – reading or having a conversation, taking a bath or going to bed earlier. I am almost a week into this change and I feel a lot better.

On Saturday morning, another thing happened which encouraged me. It was the first morning when I woke up and didn't reach for my phone. Instead, I reached for my Bible, decided to start with Matthew and read five chapters. This may sound awful, but usually I don't give my attention to reading more than a few verses, so I felt pleased. I then got up early, did jobs and prepared for the day. As I drove the children to swimming lessons, a huge rainbow appeared in the sky directly in front of me. There wasn't even any rain or showers around; it was bright sunshine and the rainbow was so vivid. I really felt that God was showing me that he was there and that he was pleased with me. Who knows if that's true, but I smiled and felt his approval of the changes.'

As this mother discovered, we are more likely to experience signs of God's presence and blessing if we take time to lift our eyes from the glowing screen and be present in the moment. And it is as we look up that we will find God patiently waiting to catch our gaze.

PAUSE TO CONSIDER:

- *How aware are you of the time you spend on your phone, social media, and other technology?*

- *What habits have you slipped into that you would like to change?*

- *How would it feel to have half a day or even half an hour totally tech-free?*

- *How would you like to put boundaries around your tech time in a day, or in a week?*

CHAPTER 9

CREATING RHYTHMS AND ROUTINES

> ... except for slight variations our routine was the same every day:
> an early morning walk, followed by [Elsa's] midday slumber close
> to me by our tree on the river bank. This lasted until teatime, then
> came our afternoon stroll.[48]

It is the last week of Jesus' life. He has just celebrated the Passover
meal with his friends, and now they leave the safety of the upper
room and make their way across the city, where Jesus continues
to teach them all they need to know for what lies ahead. Perhaps,
as they walk through the narrow streets, they see the Temple, its
gate adorned with an enormous golden vine laden with clusters of
grapes, an evocative image of Israel as God's vineyard. And perhaps
it is against this backdrop that Jesus makes one of his most famous
declarations:

> *'I am the true vine and my Father is the gardener ... Remain in*
> *me, as I also remain in you. No branch can bear fruit by itself;*
> *it must remain in the vine. Neither can you bear fruit unless*
> *you remain in me.'*

JOHN 15:1, 4

The word Jesus uses for remaining or abiding is the Greek word
menō. It is the everyday word used by the first disciples when they
asked Jesus, 'Where are you staying?' (John 1:38) and when we read
that Jesus 'stayed' in Capernaum (John 2:12). It is best translated
'live in' or 'make a home in'. This word is mentioned no less than ten

---

48 Joy Adamson, *Born Free* (Pantheon Books, 1960), p106.

times in the following verses, which I think requires us to sit up and take notice.

The Message translation puts it like this:

> *Live in me. Make your home in me just as I do in you. In the same way that a branch can't bear grapes by itself but only by being joined to the vine, you can't bear fruit unless you are joined with me.*
>
> JOHN 15:4 (MSG)

The message is clear. Just as in the right conditions and with the right support, vines will naturally bear fruit, the natural outcome of making our home in God is obedient, fruitful discipleship.

The Psalms give us a glimpse into the fact that David knew something of the secret of this. In Psalm 16 he writes: 'I have set the LORD continually before me; Because He is at my right hand, I will not be shaken' (Psalm 16:8, NASB). If, as a shepherd, soldier and king, David could set the Lord continually before him, what could it look like for us to do that in the context of our everyday lives as parents, teachers, artists, baristas, bankers, builders, farmers, nurses, students, technicians, church leaders, gardeners …?

I sometimes write in a little coastal cottage. From the upstairs window I can see across the bay, and on a clear day I can watch the sun dancing on a patch of golden sand on an ancient monastic island. Monks first came here in the sixth century, and carrying the torch of this monastic heritage, a community of Cistercian monks continue to pursue their vocation there today. Whenever we have taken the little boat to visit the island, I have been struck by the wonderful variety of wildlife: cormorants perched on rocks with their wings spread out to dry, seals frolicking in the waves on the shore, rare black swans on the lake, swallows and pheasants, and red squirrels in the trees. But as well as this gift of creation, there is something else about the place. There is a deep peace and tranquillity, not just in the sacred spaces of the monastic buildings, but in the very soil of the island itself. Every part feels like what the Celtic Christians called 'a thin space' – those rare places 'where the distance between Heaven and earth is compressed'[49] and the presence of God feels more tangible.

I found a clue to the source of this deep sense of peace on a well-worn piece of paper pinned nonchalantly with a bent drawing pin onto the chapel door. It set out the times for the monks to stop what they were doing and turn their hearts to God in prayer. It reads:

3.30am *Vigils*
6.00am *Lauds*
6.45am *Holy Mass*
8.50am *Terce*
12.15pm *Sext*
2.20pm *None*
5.30pm *Vespers*
7.35pm *Compline*

Another timetable added meals, times of work and study, reading and prayer to the schedule.

As I compared my busy and often distracted existence to this simple rhythm of prayer, something in my spirit stirred. While I wasn't sure I'd be setting my alarm for 3.15am, I knew there was something I could learn from the rhythm of this way of life.

The timetable was part of what monastic communities call A Rule of Life. Throughout the history of monasticism, beginning with the Desert Fathers and Mothers, Rules of Life have guided individuals and communities in their discipleship to Jesus. In his book *The Vision and the Vow*, Pete Greig explains:

> A Rule of Life is a set of principles and practices we build into the rhythm of our daily lives, helping us to deepen our relationship with God and to serve him more faithfully. If Creeds are what we believe

49 Eric Weiner, *Man Seeks God: My Flirtations with the Divine* (Twelve, 2012), p66.

and Christ is why we believe, a Rule is how we seek to live out that faith, day to day as disciples in the power of the Holy Spirit.[50]

A Rule of Life is essentially an agreed rhythm of practices and values which help us deepen our intimacy with God, and grow in our service to others. It has been said that we achieve inner peace when our schedule is aligned with our values. A Rule of Life is simply a means to that end.

If you are someone like me who likes structure, following a Rule of Life might be an attractive proposition; but for many, the word 'rule' can sound restrictive and legalistic, so it needs some unpacking. It is Rule (singular) not a set of rules (plural) and it comes from the word *regula* from which we get the word 'ruler' (the kind in your pencil case). The same word can be translated to mean 'trellis'.

Most marriages have a few areas where the couple knows that if they aren't careful, sparks can fly. For Richard and me this includes: the correct way to load (and unload) the dishwasher; putting up (and taking down) a tent; haircuts (cost on the one hand and failure to notice when there's been a visit to the salon on the other); and gardening – in particular our approach to pruning. Neither of us are budding Monty Dons, but we are fortunate to have a garden and we do try to keep the weeds at bay. Richard likes it to look neat and tidy whereas I prefer a more overgrown, country vibe. And so it was that Richard took it upon himself to prune back our honeysuckle that had sprawled across the patio. I had agreed to this course of action but imagined a little trim would do the job. Instead, he gave the plant a #0 on the clippers – what barbers might term a 'bald fade'. As the sweepings were relegated to the green bin, I confess it was not the finest hour of our marriage. But Richard was unrepentant and undeterred. He had googled what to do and was confident that if he tied what remained of the plant to a trellis, not only would it grow back, but it would grow back well supported and stronger. Suffice it to say, he was right.

50 'Why a Rule of Life?', *OMS*, orderofthemustardseed.com (accessed 10 March 2023).

In the same way that a trellis gives structure and support to a plant, helping it to grow, a Rule of Life can be a framework for support and growth in our spiritual lives.

We are all different, so it is important to craft a Rule of Life to suit our individual personalities, temperaments and seasons of life. The aim is always for it to provide support in our journey of discipleship and transformation, but the detail will change and develop over the seasons. I have seen Rules of Life as infographics and spreadsheets, scribbled down in notebooks and on the back of envelopes, and in beautifully designed bound folders, as abstract drawings or neatly ruled … the choice is yours. The most important thing is to create a gospel-centred, living document in a way that works for you.

St Benedict, the founder of the Benedictine monastic community, is famous for his Rule of Life which brought together the best monastic wisdom of his day. It remains a key document that later generations of monks have used to guide them in applying the gospel to life in community. Benedict's desire was that the Rule was to be applied from the heart, and he saw it as 'not a series of prescribed actions but a series of opening doors.'[51] In his Prologue, he expresses his wish that:

> … through the continual practice of monastic observance and the life of faith, our hearts are opened wide, and the way of God's commandments is run in a sweetness of love that is beyond words.[52]

Benedict doesn't deal in lofty moral concepts. Much of his Rule involves ordering the practical things of life, because he believed that in a well-ordered community it is easier to make time and space for God.

Benedict's Rule of Life was about finding God in the ordinary, the commonplace and unspectacular, and in so doing, practising

51 Saint Benedict Abbot of Monte Cristo, *The Rule of Saint Benedict* (Gracewing, 2003), pxviii.
52 Ibid.

the way of Jesus and being formed into people of love. It is wisdom not just for sixth-century monks, but for us on our journey as disciples of Jesus today.

If we are seeking to be transformed into people whose lives reflect the way of Jesus, how we spend our time matters – because it is the things that we invest in and give our attention to that influence and shape the people we become. And looking at how Jesus lived is not a bad place to start.

C.S. Lewis writes:

> Our imitation of God in this life – that is, our willed imitation as distinct from any of the likenesses which he has impressed upon our natures or states – must be an imitation of God incarnate: our model is the Jesus, not only of Calvary, but of the workshop, the roads, the crowds, the clamorous demands and surly oppositions, the lack of all peace and privacy, the interruptions. For this, so strangely unlike anything we can attribute to the Divine life in itself, is apparently not only like, but is, the Divine life operating under human conditions.[53]

Time and again we read that Jesus made time to be alone with God – going out early in the morning and late at night, up mountains and into olive gardens to pray. He prayed with his friends and in the synagogues. Jesus encouraged the disciples to come away with him after a time of active mission. He also took plenty of time to celebrate and enjoy a good party, as well as enjoying meals with tax collectors and friends.

Author and prayer director Jill Weber advises that we draw up a Rule of Life in two stages.

STAGE 1 - INVENTORY:

Make a list of the habits and practices that are already in your life and shape you (for good and ill!). For example, having your phone

---

53 C.S. Lewis, *The Four Loves* (Geoffrey Bles, 1960), p4.

by the bed, watching Netflix late into the night, regularly meeting up with friends to pray, taking a lunch break.

STAGE 2 - INVITATION:

Consider which practices you feel you may need to stop. And only then, which ones to take up. Perhaps it might be deciding to keep your phone out of the bedroom, to welcome God as the first thing you do each day and last thing you do at night, to get more sleep or to include a weekly prayer walk in your lunchtime routine.

Remember to keep it simple and craft it in a way that works for you. We will come from different walks of life and have different traditions and practices to build on – there is no right or wrong. It's a living document that you can return to and revise time and again.

Dusting off some old journals, I was surprised (and delighted) to discover not only the duration of my propensity for black Moleskine notebooks, but also that although I hadn't, in those days, heard of the concept of a Rule of Life, finding a trellis for 'abiding' was something for which I'd been searching for many years. In some early musings, I'd written a list of things I wanted to change including:

- Living life 'on the run'.
- Living off other people's experiences of God.
- Existing with 'one-inch deep' spirituality.
- Not being intentional in pursuing Jesus.

On the same page, I expressed my desire to move from a 'tip of the iceberg' spirituality to one that truly transforms. I wanted to learn how to make space to pay attention to God throughout the day. A scribbled prayer followed:

'Lord God, I want to grow deeper in my "backstage" so I have more to offer on the "front stage". I want to intentionally

slow down, and in all the distractions and busyness of my life to create space, to enjoy being in your presence rather than rushing ahead; to find moments when "deep calls to deep"; to bathe in the ocean of your love, not just experience it drop by drop. This is my heart. Help me to find a way.'

I still have a long way to go, but, in his kindness, I can see ways that God has been answering that prayer.

My role at Care for the Family involves speaking at the Christian summer festivals and, in doing so, it has been a delight to engage with some of the team from the organization 24-7 Prayer. This connection took Richard and me on a journey to explore an expression of discipleship through one of the 24-7 streams. The Order of the Mustard Seed is an ecumenical, lay-led, dispersed missional community, anchored in the local church and united by a shared Rule of Life. Those who use the popular Lectio 365 devotional app will be familiar with the OMS' six practices – creativity, prayer, justice, hospitality, learning and mission.

So for me, it made sense to ground my Rule of Life in these six practices. I drew six boxes, one for each of the practices, and then jotted down habits and practices I could adopt that would give support and structure for my spiritual journey. But in my enthusiasm, I set the bar much too high. Each box contained new things that I was keen to adopt. But there are only so many hours in the day and only so many new things we have the capacity for. Rather than being a life-giving trellis of support and an easy yoke, my Rule of Life felt like a weight to carry. I consigned it to the recycling bin and started again.

This time I began by writing down the things I already did from time to time that were life-giving. I resolved to do them more regularly and to incorporate them as a regular rhythm in my life. And working from the premise that there is no sacred/secular divide, I made these practices all-encompassing. So as well as rhythms of prayer, in the 'creativity' box I included calligraphy and bread-making (a short-lived activity!). Under 'hospitality' I included how we used our home, as well as time for rest and reflection. I have focused on different practices at different times and added to them as appropriate. Starting small and making a few small changes that I've been able to build on over the years has been the best way forward.

And my experience of a Rule of Life is that far from being a list of obligations that drain, the opposite is true. If we take time to discover the practices that work with our personality and our lifestyle, they feed our soul and bring life.

The principle behind a Rule of Life is summed up well in this old folktale:

An old man was talking with his grandson. 'Inside me there are two wolves,' he told the boy. 'One wolf is good and does no harm. He is filled with kindness, patience, faithfulness and hope. But the other wolf is bad. He is full of bitterness, anger, resentment, regret, impatience and greed. All day long they battle against each other and at times the fight is furious.'

The little boy's eyes were wide. 'But Grandfather,' he asked, 'which one wins?'

The old man pulled the boy close and whispered in his ear: 'The one I feed.'

PAUSE TO CONSIDER:

- *Are there any practices that you would like to introduce into the rhythm of your day that might deepen your intimacy with God?*

- *What, for you, is life-giving? Can you incorporate any of these things into the rhythm of your life?*

CHAPTER 10

ENJOYING THE THINGS THAT BRING LIFE

> [The Adamsons were uniquely able to train a lioness] ... not by any deliberate attempt to do so, but merely by allowing the animal to grow up in their company and *never* allowing her nature to be subjected to the strains of being confined in any way.[54]

During a busy season of work shortly after Richard and I got married, we had the opportunity to head out of town for the weekend. No phone calls, no appointments, no demanding clients, just the two of us. I couldn't wait!

We threw a couple of overnight bags in the car, took a deep breath to savour the moment, turned on the ignition and set off down the road. We were driving my much-loved blue Mini, a car which had served us well over the years, running the gauntlet between Bristol and Birmingham in the early days of our relationship. One of the quirky features of this little car was the music system – a CD player in the boot which had to be primed with a maximum of five CDs before beginning the journey. I enjoy listening to worship music and decided that playing worship songs on the journey would set the weekend up nicely. My preparation for the trip had therefore included loading the player with five carefully chosen CDs to send us on our way.

Congratulating ourselves that against the odds we had made the getaway, we settled into the journey and I leant forward to press play. But to my surprise, instead of the dulcet tones of Tim Hughes, Chris Tomlin or Delirious coming from the speakers balanced precariously

---

54 Joy Adamson, *Born Free* (Pantheon Books, 1960), pxi.

on the back seat, came the unmistakeable voice of Bruce Springsteen. Before leaving, Richard had inspected my CDs and jettisoned them in favour of his own. While at one level there was nothing wrong with his selection – which also included Elton John and Queen – I had to confess that I was irritated at this unwarranted intervention. 'What could be better,' I asked, 'than setting off on our weekend with 'How Great is Our God' ringing in our ears?' Richard's reply floored me. He didn't really like listening to worship music and it certainly wouldn't be his music of choice for the journey ahead. I couldn't grasp his thinking. How could anyone not want to listen to worship music in the car? And I am ashamed to say that in that moment I honestly doubted that he was even a Christian.

My older (and wiser) self now sees things a little differently. There was nothing flaky about Richard's faith. He simply doesn't particularly prioritize listening to worship music. While, for me, that is an important way of enjoying and even deepening my relationship with God, for Richard there are other ways. He loves the world of ideas and concepts and for him, faith is to be understood as much as experienced; he engages his mind as well as his heart.

I had confused personality and spirituality.

Spirituality is not a 'one size fits all'. God has made each one of us unique, and we can each learn to grow in our relationship with him, working with the grain of our individual personalities. The Myers-Briggs is perhaps one of the best-known psychometric tests and has paved the way for many other psychological questionnaires based on numbers, shapes, colours, letters, animals or a myriad of other classifications, all of which seek to help shed light on what makes us tick. Some personality tests are better researched and more reliable than others, but they can be a useful tool in helping us to grow in self-awareness, understand our strengths, and recognize the things that hold us back.

The story of the shepherd boy David taking on the giant Goliath has something to teach us in this context. The Bible tells us that the

Philistines had gathered their forces for war and set up camp on one hill, with the Israelites on the hill opposite and a valley in between. Morning and evening for forty days the nine-foot-tall Goliath had mocked the Israelites, challenging them to combat, but no one in the Israelite camp had been willing to take him on. That was until David arrives on an errand to deliver food to his brothers on the front line. Hearing Goliath's taunts, David boldly offers to respond to the challenge, and is brought to King Saul who reluctantly agrees to his request.

In an effort to give David the best chance of survival, Saul orders the royal armour to be given to him. Servants bring it in, and glinting in the sunlight, it is magnificent. They dress David in the tunic, fasten the iron breastplate around his chest, and put the bronze helmet on his head. Finally, he is handed the royal sword. The Bible says:

> David fastened on his sword over the tunic and tried walking around ... 'I cannot go in these,' he said to Saul, 'because I am not used to them.' So he took them off. Then he took his staff in his hand, chose five smooth stones from the stream, put them in the pouch of his shepherd's bag and, with his sling in his hand, approached the Philistine.

1 SAMUEL 17:39–40

As the first stone left the leather sling, it was all over for the giant.

Saul's armour fitted the king well; it looked good on him, and it was what he needed for battle. But David was different. While keeping his father's sheep, he'd become skilled at using his sling to kill lions and bears, but when he wore the armour that fitted Saul so well, it was cumbersome and unwieldy; it weighed him down. If David had worn it, it would have been game over for him.

In learning how to work with our personalities and play to our strengths, we need to resist the temptation of putting on 'Saul's armour' – or allowing others to put it on us. Jesus said: 'I won't lay anything heavy or ill-fitting on you' (Matthew 11:30, MSG). And if Jesus won't put it on us, why would we put it on ourselves?

The key in our spiritual journey is to develop habits, patterns and practices that work *with* our character and don't rub against it. In later chapters, we will explore practical things we can do that will help us make good progress. Some of these practices will suit our personality; they'll bring us life and we'll find them relatively easy and enjoyable. Others we need to recognize as Saul's armour – they are not a good fit for us.

I am someone who thrives on routine. I've had almost the same thing for breakfast for the last thirty years, and the lunch I take to work looks remarkably similar each day. Perhaps it's no surprise then that when, as a child, my mother gave me some Bible-reading notes, I found it relatively easy to slot into the routine of reading them – it didn't require too much effort. And the result was that day by day I became familiar with the Scriptures and, more than that, I learnt to love the God who was revealed in them.

I confess that on occasions I felt a little bit proud of my regime, but a conversation with a friend revealed that this sense of pride was ill-placed. My definition of what constituted a 'good' devotional time was formulaic and small-minded. My friend is free and easy-going; she loves spontaneity and hates routine. Every month when she was young, her godmother sent her a set of Bible-reading notes, which she endeavoured to plough through at night. But she found them dry and boring, and the monotony drained her. Added to that, she was weighed down by a sense of guilt, comparing herself to those who carried out the 'quiet time' routine with ease. Looking back, what she (and I) had missed was that reading Bible notes by rote every night, while obviously not a bad thing to do, did not necessarily make you more spiritual. The aim wasn't to achieve an unbroken streak of daily Bible-reading. Something bigger was at stake. The ultimate goal was getting to know and love God – in this case, by meeting him in his word.

My friend commented:

'When I grasped what Bible-reading was really about, it was a lightbulb moment! I'd been focusing on the wrong thing. It wasn't about religiously ticking off prescribed readings but discovering how to read my Bible in a time and place that worked for me. I began to read the Bible on the train, to listen to it in the car, and to browse through a psalm in the bath. Everything changed. Instead of it being a boring obligation, it became life-giving in my relationship with God.'

As author A.W. Tozer cautions:

The whole transaction of religious conversion has been made mechanical and spiritless … We have almost forgotten that God is a person and, as such, can be cultivated as any person can.[55]

Author Gary Thomas takes up this theme in his book *Sacred Pathways* as he explores the various ways we can grow in our love for God in line with our personality. Studying characters from Scripture and the history of the church's varied traditions, he uncovers many different ways of finding intimacy with God. Our personality and temperament mean that we will inevitably be more comfortable with some expressions than others, and it's important to identify which best suit us and bring us delight and connection with God.

A word of warning: we mustn't throw the baby out with the bathwater. Most of us will naturally gravitate to the expressions of faith and spiritual practices that align with our personality. But this is not pick 'n' mix. It's not about custom-fitting our discipleship to our personality. If we are to grow into wholeness, we may have to learn to pay attention to ways of spiritual engagement that don't come so naturally to us.

Extroverts may have developed a highly socialized spirituality, loving to spend time praying and worshipping with others but, in

---

55 A.W. Tozer, *The Pursuit of God* (Christian Publications, 1980), p12–13.

so doing, perhaps neglecting times of quiet reflection that could bring a richness and depth to their journey. And introverts may be faced with the equal and opposite problem. They prefer the individualistic approach of contemplation and solitude, but neglect being in community. It may take some work, but to prevent becoming lopsided in our spiritual growth, we must learn to cultivate practices that aren't as familiar to us.

Since lockdown, most mornings Richard and I join a morning Zoom call for a short time of prayer with others from around the world. By the wonders of technology, a faithful band gather to pray from different time zones, dressed for the office, clad in Lycra en route to the gym, or still in pyjamas or pink fluffy dressing gowns – anything goes! Over time, we have learnt to pray in new and creative ways. Each day is led by a different person, who brings their own unique way of connecting with God. Two of these practices in particular have taken me outside my comfort zone. The first was to spend time looking at a painting and use it as a springboard for prayer. To my initial surprise, the picture was not generally a religious work of art but more the type of thing you would see at the Tate Modern. Since then, photographs of inner city parks, graffiti, abstract art and sculptures have all inspired my prayers.

The second experience was time set aside to pray in the quiet. When my friend Moira told me she was going to lead half an hour of silent prayer, I knew that for my personality this would be a challenge. And I wasn't far wrong! As she gently guided us through the first week, I battled to tether my mind to the present. One day, after what seemed an eternity, I was certain we would be coming in to land and sneaked a look at my watch to find we had only been going for five minutes! But while I will never find this easy, as the weeks have gone by, I have come to love and appreciate the stillness.

The Bible is full of metaphors which emphasize that we need to put in some effort to grow in our Christian walk. In his letters to the New Testament churches, Paul refers to the discipline and perseverance required by soldiers, farmers, and especially athletes. So as vital as it is to discover the freedom of practices that work *with* our personality and don't drain us, we also need to pay attention to those that may be outside our comfort zone but ultimately will help us.

In researching for my parenting book *A Mind of Their Own*, I was fascinated to discover how much the Bible's teaching about spiritual formation is mirrored in what scientists have discovered about the brain. The neuropsychological theory that 'neurons that fire together wire together' (a phrase coined by psychologist Donald Hebb in 1949) helps us understand how it works. Every time we do or respond to something, neurons in our brain are activated in a particular order, creating a pathway between the parts of the brain that are involved. And because the brain is a pattern-seeking device, the next time we do the same activity, our neurons are stimulated to follow the same pattern. When we repeat the activity, we will find it easier; and the time after that, it will be easier still and so on.

This analogy may help. Imagine you are trying to walk across an overgrown field. You have to fight your way through tall grasses, ferns, weeds and brambles. It's hard work, but eventually you make it to the other side. The next day you repeat the walk and this time, because you flattened some of the undergrowth the day before, the field is a little easier to cross. The following day, it's easier still. Eventually, by walking it again and again, you make a clear, wide path.

In the same way, the more we do something the more it will become ingrained as a habit – and this is the case in the area of spiritual disciplines as much as in any other area of life. What scientists call the 'plasticity of the brain' (the ability of our brain to change and grow), the Bible calls 'the renewal of our mind' (Romans 12:2). And with practice, we can learn new ways or spiritual exercises to deepen our faith, to pursue the attentive stillness of the lioness and cooperate with the Holy Spirit as he forms us more into the image of Christ.

PAUSE TO CONSIDER:

- *Are you 'wearing' anything heavy or ill-fitting, whether it is something that you have chosen yourself or that someone else has put on you?*

- *Do you know what suits you, what fits you well? What brings you delight and connection with God?*

CHAPTER 11

BEING ATTENTIVE IN
THE MOMENT

Later she returned to George's tent for a few moments, put her paw affectionately round him and moaned softly, as if to say to him: 'You know that I love you, but I have a friend outside to whom I simply *must* go. I hope you will understand.'[56]

In my role at Care for the Family, I work closely with Rob Parsons, our chairman and founder. We are regularly on the road together on Care for the Family speaking tours or at Christian festivals, so I have first-hand experience of how often people want to speak to him. There have been many occasions when we have been heading from green room to meeting venue at an event and someone has stepped across his path or touched his arm and asked to have a word. And time and again I have watched Rob stop – even if just for a moment – to respond to the interruption and give that person the dignity of time and attention.

The problem with living full and busy lives means that we can easily get preoccupied with our own needs and simply don't have any capacity for interruptions. If we read the Gospels, we see that Jesus was always interruptible. In fact, many of his miracles took place as the result of an interruption. On the way to healing Jairus' daughter, Jesus is interrupted by a sick woman, but he stops to heal her (Mark 5:22–43). When he is journeying to Jerusalem for the final Passover, he is interrupted by Bartimaeus, but he stops to restore the blind man's sight (Mark 10:46–52). Teaching at a house in Capernaum, he is interrupted by some men who make a

---

56 Joy Adamson, *Born Free* (Pantheon Books, 1960), p116.

hole in the roof to lower their paralyzed friend down to him. Jesus stops mid-message and heals him (Mark 2:1–12). Whatever the interruption, it seems that Jesus was able to set his own agenda to one side and be present to whatever was going on in the moment.

We all have interruptions in our day: the immediate practical needs of children, colleagues stopping by our workstation for a chat, a friend needing a lift to the garage, or the need of a stranger in crisis. Interruptions are a part of life. And rather than pressing on with our own agenda, if we are prepared to respond to them, we can find that God meets us there.

When making calculations, statisticians add in a 'margin for error' – an allowance for possible mistakes or changes without them having a damaging effect on the final result. And we would perhaps do well, where possible, to live our lives with a 'margin for error'. Instead of overloading our schedules, we can build in time for the possibility of delays, for things to go wrong, and especially for interruptions.

This was something my parents did well when I was growing up – they were known for allowing plenty of time. My siblings and I would be the first to be dropped off and the first to be picked up from school and parties; we'd be first in line for cinema tickets; and our parents would always leave the house with an eternity of time in which to get to the train station just in case we 'met cows in the road'. (The journey to the nearest station involved passing a farm, and while we did, on one occasion, get stopped by cows, by no stretch of the imagination was it a likely scenario!) My parents were always early. And I hated it. Years of being the first to leave the party and hours spent 'wasting time' on train platforms meant that once I was in charge of my own schedule, I decided I would never be early for anything again.

But several years on and a history of missed buses and trains caught by the skin of my teeth, I understood the wisdom of their ways. At Care for the Family, we often quote the mantra: 'It's very difficult to be on time, but it's easy to be early!' When we travel to London, our protocol is to catch the train before the one that will get us there on time. When all goes smoothly, that means there can be some hanging around in coffee shops at the other end before the meeting starts. But if there are roadworks on the way to the station, a signal failure, the Tube line is down, Google Maps takes us in the wrong direction, or I have simply not left enough time and missed the first train, we don't need to fret that we will be late for the meeting. We have learnt to add a margin for error into our schedules and our lives are better for it.

A famous psychology study took place at Princeton Theological Seminary, New Jersey, in the early 1970s involving a group of students training to become ministers.[57] They were invited to prepare a talk on the parable of the Good Samaritan and, after doing so, were told that they needed to walk to a nearby recording studio to deliver their sermon. The participants were then randomly told one of three conditions: i) that they had plenty of time, and were early; ii) that they were on time, but should head over now so as not to be late; or iii) that they were running late and needed to hurry. The route involved walking through a narrow alley, and as part of the experiment, an actor was slumped in a doorway, head down, eyes closed, not moving. Each subject made the journey on their own, and as they passed by, the stranger coughed and groaned, clearly in need of help.

The soon-to-be priests, having just prepared a talk about a very similar scenario to the one they were now experiencing, responded in different ways. When the researchers analysed this, the results were fascinating. They found that 63% of those who were told they were early stopped to help rather than passing on by; 45% of those who were told they were on time did likewise; and only 10% of

57 J.M. Darley and C.D. Batson (1973). 'From Jerusalem to Jericho: A study of situational and dispositional variables in helping behavior', *Journal of Personality and Social Psychology*, 27(1), pp100–108.

those who thought they were late stopped to help. Overall, the key external factor that determined whether or not they stopped to help was how much of a hurry they were in!

Making time for others becomes harder when we live in a pressurized way. When we pack our calendars full and fail to leave any unscheduled time in our day, we limit our options. When faced with an interruption, we have to choose between responding to it or meeting other goals. But if we build in a 'margin for error' we can broaden our attention and be available not just to the needs of others but especially to God's presence in our lives.

Intentionally living life with margins is a great way to recover that white space in our calendar. Instead of running from pillar to post, we are able to have moments, both spontaneous and planned, when we can orient our hearts to God.

I recently came across Ronald Rolheiser's lovely little book *Domestic Monastery*, inspired by the routines and rhythms of the monks. As I turned the pages, I realized that if I'd come across his wisdom as a young mother, a huge burden would have lifted from my shoulders.

He tells the story of Carlo Carretto, one of the leading spiritual writers of the twentieth century. Carretto spent many years praying in the Sahara Desert by himself, but one day when he returned to Italy to visit his mother, he had a startling insight. He realized that for more than thirty years his mother had been busy raising a family with little or no time to herself, yet she was more contemplative than he was.

It was not that there was anything wrong with spending that time praying in the desert; it was, rather, that there was something very right about what his mother had been doing – living an interrupted life in the melee of the incessant demands of small children. Putting their needs before her own in that season of her life had shaped her character and enlarged her capacity for love.

A monastery is a place set apart, a place in which to learn the value of powerlessness and, in particular, to learn that time is not ours but God's. Carretto came to the wonderful conclusion that 'he had been in a monastery, but so had she'.[58]

It is worth remembering that monasteries were places of work and enterprise – beekeeping, brewing, and building were among the tasks carried out by the monks as well as time spent in study and prayer. The ringing of a bell at regular times was the monks' summons to immediately stop whatever they were doing – writing a letter, gardening, studying, praying, sleeping – and turn their minds to the activity the bell was now calling them to. It was a reminder to look beyond their own agenda to God's agenda, and to remember his presence in their lives.

Like Carlo Carretto's mother, parents of young children will know what it's like to feel the equivalent of that monastic bell at all times of the day and night; the interruptions of young children calling us to stop what we are doing and reminding us that our time isn't our own. But whatever season of life we are in, we can use the interruptions to teach us this lesson and help pivot our hearts to God's living presence. Rolheiser writes:

> During all the most active years of our lives we are reminded daily, sometimes hourly, that time is not our own; we are monks practising a demanding asceticism. There will not always be time to smell the flowers, and we are not always poorer for that fact. Monasticism has its own spiritual payoffs. To be forced to work, to be tied down with duties, to have to get up early, to have little time to call your own, to be burdened with the responsibility of children and the demands of debts and mortgages, to go to bed exhausted after a working day is to be in touch with our humanity. It is too an opportunity to recognize that time is not our own …
>
> Most important, recognizing in our duties and pressure the sound of the monastic bell actually helps us to smell the flowers, to give each instant of our lives the time it deserves – and not

58 Ronald Rolheiser, *Domestic Monastery* (Darton, Longman & Todd, 2019), p17.

necessarily the time I feel like giving it … These are monastic secrets worth knowing.[59]

Another monastic secret worth knowing was taught to us by the seventeenth-century monk, Brother Lawrence. Born Nicholas Herman in French Lorraine, he served briefly as a footman and soldier and then became a lay brother in the Carmelite order in Paris in 1666. He had a remarkable conversion when he was just eighteen. The sight of a bare tree in the snow on a winter's day kindled in his heart a deep wonder at the arrival of spring and the power of God to bring renewal and change. From that moment he grew in the knowledge and love of God, seeking each day 'to walk as in his presence'.[60] He worked humbly in the monastery kitchen for fifteen years and learnt to find the presence of God as much in his kitchen duties, washing the pots and pans, as in the set times of prayer:

> The time of business does not with me differ from the time of prayer; and in the noise and clutter of my kitchen, while several persons are at the same time calling for different things, I possess God in as great tranquillity as if I were upon my knees at the Blessed Sacrament.[61]

He describes the secret as learning to pay 'simple attention' to God in all things:

> I make it my business only to persevere in his holy presence, wherein I keep myself by a simple attention, and a general fond regard to God, which I may call an *actual presence* of God; or, to speak better, an habitual, silent, and secret conversation of the soul with God.[62]

Learning the secret of finding the presence of God in all things may be a challenge if our lives are full of complexity. But redirecting

59 Ibid, p82.
60 Brother Lawrence, *The Practice of the Presence of God: Being the Conversations and Letters of Nicholas Herman of Lorraine* (Jove Publications, 1958), p29.
61 Ibid, p8.
62 Ibid, p36.

our attention to God in whatever we are doing in the moment will mean that we live in such a way that we are open to his presence throughout every day.

As many of us are combining a variety of roles during the working week, the conventional 80,000 hours of work through our lifetime (40 hours x 50 weeks x 40 years) may no longer be the norm. But, however many hours or activities we consider 'work', it is by definition a considerable chunk of our lives. In this context, attending to God in the moment could mean paying attention to the work we are doing and consciously offering it to God as worship. It could be that we use our imagination to visualize Jesus entering our workplace and walking around. As we see him in our mind's eye, we could ask ourselves: what would he notice? Or it could be that we use a 'prayer of examen' at the end of the day to notice where God was at work, or what we missed, or what he might draw our attention to. If we stop to consider the possibilities, they are endless.

One of our sons and our daughter-in-law spent a couple of years working at the St Stephen's Society in Hong Kong, the extraordinary ministry set up by Jackie Pullinger over fifty years ago. The Society exists to preach the gospel, reach the poor and see people set free from all kinds of addictions through faith in Jesus Christ. Those who serve there live with 'the Brothers', and journey with them as they are healed and learn what it is to follow him. The road to freedom from addiction can present its own joys and challenges and can be a masterclass in learning that our time isn't our own.

One couple who had worked there for a number of years spoke about some of the challenges they faced in practising the presence of God. Residential pastoral work with drug addicts was intense and volatile. From dawn to dusk, life was hectic: there was always a problem to resolve, a fight to break up or a logistical issue to sort out. A morning quiet time was an impossible luxury, and there was very rarely a moment to retreat to a place of solitude. Silence was unimaginable! As a result, they were compelled to cultivate new ways to pray, seek the Lord and engage with the Holy Spirit.

Inspired by Brother Lawrence's secret of practising the presence of God in mundane tasks, they learnt to spend time with God in the midst of daily tasks and competing demands. They developed rhythms of prayer which coincided with daily activities. They used the Lord's Prayer to pray while doing maintenance work, interceded for particular people while doing laundry, or prayed in tongues while playing sport with the Brothers. These rhythms of prayer acted like a runway for the Holy Spirit. Some days, it was just a case of practising them as a discipline, irrespective of what happened as a result. On other days, the Lord would make his presence known in a particularly tangible way. In the end, these rhythms became second nature. Having finished their work in Hong Kong, they still continue these practices, despite being in a very different of season of life. The permanent posture of their heart is an awareness of the present and of Jesus' constant companionship.

From time to time at Care for the Family, we gather the members of the team who are involved in public speaking. It is always a rich and meaningful time, a great opportunity to share the joys and challenges of life on the stage. Storytelling is an important part of our ministry and on one occasion the discussion moved on to the subject of finding stories that conveyed a point in an impactful way. One colleague shared his secret: he walks around with a 'speaker's lens'. He makes a point of noticing the experiences of everyday life, things that many of us miss, and has discovered that they provide a mine of material for his talks.

In the same way, we can put on a lens that sharpens our focus on the presence and activity of God in our lives. As naturalist Henry David Thoreau observes, 'Heaven is under our feet as well as over our heads.'[63]

Daniel Grothe, in talking about the work of author Annie

63 Henry David Thoreau, *Walden; or Life in the Woods* (Ticknor and Fields, 1854), p178.

Dillard, describes her as providing 'our awakening to the glory that is everywhere hidden in plain sight':[64]

> Can you see it in the suburban neighbourhood? Can you feel the crackling thunder of Mount Sinai in the kindergarten carpool line? Can you see Jesus in the little baby wrapped in swaddling clothes, lying in the tiny bassinette beside your bed, ready to rouse you through every watch of the night for a few calories of breast milk? Have you ever tripped over Jacob's ladder (Genesis 28:12), ever been caught in the crossfire between heaven and earth, ever heard the song of the angels that are always ascending and descending among us? We get tired and our eyes grow faint, but it's all right there … Can you *see* it?[65]

As well as looking through a new lens to foster what has been called 'a holy wakefulness' in our lives, we can also use everyday activities to help us reorient our hearts towards God, allowing them to remind us to pause, turn our thoughts to him, and notice his activity in and around us.

One of the simplest everyday activities to harness in prayer is the act of breathing. Breath prayer is simply taking a moment to be still, to breathe deeply, and on the inhale and exhale to recite a scripture or a promise.

When I was a family lawyer, there were days when I had to respond swiftly to the needs of those who had been subjected to domestic violence, or whose children were about to be taken into care. It was in the urgency of those situations that I valued the practice of taking a moment to breathe and remember the promises of God.

Short breath prayers can embed truth in our muscle memory. One autumn when our children were little I was using an electric

64 Daniel Grothe, *The Power of Place: Choosing Stability in a Rootless Age* (Nelson Books, 2021), p117.
65 Ibid.

blower to collect fallen leaves in our garden. It was heavy to say the least, and the next day as I wheeled our youngest around the shops in his buggy, I realized I must have torn my stomach muscles more than I realized … Fast forward 24 hours and I found myself in A and E with a burst appendix. I had used a breath prayer that week from Psalm 23, and as I lay in the hospital, about to go into surgery for a potentially serious operation, those verses returned to my mind. Simply breathing 'The Lord is my shepherd; I shall not want,' over and over brought me a very real sense of God's presence and peace.

The ways in which we can use the everyday things to remind us of God's presence in and around us are limitless, but here are some ideas to start us off:

- Put a meaningful photo as a prompt on the screensaver on our phone or laptop.
- Take time to be still in God's presence while waiting for the Wi-Fi to connect.
- Pay attention to our breathing, receiving each breath as God's gift.
- Walk around the office or building as a reminder of God's hand on our work.
- Light a candle to remember Jesus as the light in the darkness.
- Use particular landmarks on a school run or commute to work as a point to welcome his presence on the journey.
- Leave a special object in our coat pocket such as a shell, button or coin as a prompt to pray.
- Read slowly and prayerfully through our diary commitments at the beginning and end of the day.
- Notice and be grateful for opportunities to serve when washing hands or using hand cream.

- Set an alarm at midday as a reminder to say the Lord's Prayer.
- Welcome God into our home while tidying bedrooms, washing up, mowing grass or doing other household chores.
- Attach a memorable object to our car keyring as a prompt to be aware of God's presence while on the road.
- Wear a special ring or piece of jewellery to remind ourselves that we belong to God.

PAUSE TO CONSIDER:

- *How do you respond to interruptions in your day?*

- *How could you build in more margin for error in your life now?*

- *Who does your time belong to? What or who would you like to give more time to?*

- *What could you use as a prompt to turn your attention to God?*

CHAPTER 12

FINDING PLACES TO RETREAT

Rain pools and shallow rivers had always excited and invigorated [Elsa], but this great ocean was a real heaven for her. She swam effortlessly, far out of her depth; ducked us and splashed water with her tail.[66]

As well as finding the opportunity to be attentive to God in spontaneous moments, we can intentionally plan specific times in our week where we create the right conditions for enjoying and experiencing his presence. But, as we have seen, we are not on a level playing field and this will take energy and resolve.

Author Elizabeth Dreyer writes:

In a profound way, our intentionality is a key ingredient determining whether we notice God everywhere or only in church or only in suffering, or nowhere. It all depends on how we choose to fashion our world.[67]

In my work at Care for the Family, I spend time supporting couples in their marriages, and it struck me that there's an analogy between the good habits that help build a relationship between couples and habits that can enrich our time with God. In the early years of our marriage, Richard and I found it relatively easy to spend time together. He would happily clear his diary to traipse around art galleries and coffee shops with me, and I didn't give a second thought to scouring cold, dirty scrapyards in search of elusive

66 Joy Adamson, *Born Free* (Pantheon Books, 1960), p29.
67 Elizabeth Dreyer, *Earth Crammed with Heaven: A Spirituality of Everyday Life* (Paulist Press, 1994), p23.

parts for his kit car. We were in love. Prioritizing time together felt effortless. And we thought it would always be like that.

But fast forward ten years and our lives looked a little different. Richard spent his days immersed in balance sheets, client meetings and strategic forecasts. At home with four small children, my day involved scraping Play-Doh off the carpet, finding missing swimming goggles, making jam tarts and marmite sandwiches, and going to the toddler group – all bookended with the daily school run. Those days were full, and by and large enjoyable, but little by little, we began living parallel lives. It wasn't a decision we made; it was more just a way of life that we drifted into – something that has been described as a 'creeping separateness'.[68] It might have gone on like that for some time, but wise friends encouraged us to change course by scheduling in our diary a regular time together, a time where we could connect and be there just for each other. A time not for folding the laundry, doing the ironing or catching up with emails, but a time just to be together.

Over the years, our 'date night' has looked different and we have had to be flexible. Sometimes it has been glorious, other times a disaster. And there have been weeks when it has slipped by the wayside. But the important thing is that more often than not, it happened, and regularity of time together has woven into our relationship over the course of a lifetime. And not only that – our love has grown because of it.

The principle of setting aside time for each other also comes into play when I am on the road – somehow it seems that our diaries are always mutually exclusive! I am free during the day when Richard is at work, and by the time he is back home, I am about to do the sound check at the event venue. So we have had to be creative about connecting with each other – first thing in the morning, over breakfast (me), and on the way to work (Richard). When I

68 Sheldon Vanauken, *A Severe Mercy* (Hodder and Stoughton, 1977), p37.

share with couples the principle of scheduling in regular time alone with each other, sometimes there is pushback. Some protest that intentionally putting this in the diary smacks of duty or legalism, but I always give them the same response: 'Sometimes it is the duty of love to make time. Making time creates the right conditions for love to flourish.'

And if that is true in a marriage, then how much more could it be true of our relationship with God? What difference could it make if we planned, prioritized and protected some time in our week for friendship with him? If we chose his company above the other things that demand our time simply because we enjoy uninterrupted time in his presence?

'Strategic withdrawal' is a military term used to describe the decision to retreat from the front line of battle in order to regroup and regain perspective. And as battle-weary followers of Jesus, we would do well to build into our lives times of strategic withdrawal, or at the very least occasional moments of retreat from the front line of battle.

Jesus is our example in this. We read in the Gospels that 'Jesus often withdrew to lonely places and prayed' (Luke 5:16). Time and again, he would intentionally retreat from the demands of the crowds to linger undisturbed in his Father's presence. As Charles Spurgeon writes: 'The Sun of Righteousness was up before the sun.'[69] Time with his Father was Jesus' first priority.

Pastor Rick Warren coined a mantra to encourage us to build uninterrupted time with Jesus by 'diverting daily, withdrawing weekly, and abandoning annually.'[70] It's a helpful strategy that allows us to get away from the clamour of the everyday, and to

---

69 C.H. Spurgeon, 'First Forgiveness, Then Healing' in *The Metropolitan Tabernacle Pulpit Sermons*, vol. 41 (London: Passmore & Alabaster, 1895), pp286–287.
70 Rick Warren, 'What to do when you want to give up', *Biblical Leadership* 26, August 2019, biblicalleadership.com (accessed 23 March 2023).

intentionally withdraw into God's presence, reset our priorities and regain our perspective.

Let's take a closer look at this:

DIVERT DAILY

There have been seasons in my life when the relentless demands of the workplace have meant hardly any time to come up for air. There was a time when the only way I could 'divert' from the onslaught of small children was to lock myself in the bathroom for a few minutes. At other times, the barrage of issues whirring round my head meant that it was hard to focus on anything meaningful. But however busy I am, I generally find that I make time for the things I want to do – shower, eat, drink coffee and chat to my husband or children. And while I believe, in theory, that making time for God is top of my priority list, it doesn't just happen. I need to plan it.

At the moment life is full, but I have a degree of control over my day, and I have discovered the value of a regular rhythm of simply turning to God three times a day: first thing in the morning, at lunchtime and, even if just for a moment, at the end of the day.

God's people beat the drum of a daily prayer rhythm throughout Scripture. In the Psalms, David cries out to God 'evening, morning and noon' (Psalm 55:17). In defiance against King Nebuchadnezzar's edict that no one pray to anyone except himself, Daniel knelt before an open window to pray to God three times a day (Daniel 6:10). In Acts, we read that 'Peter and John were going up to the temple at the time of prayer – at three in the afternoon' (Acts 3:1). And it was during the midday time of prayer when Cornelius called for Peter (Acts 10:9). A daily prayer rhythm was part of the life of the Temple and the Early Church, and it is a rhythm that works for me. It is not perfect, but it is a start. It helps to tether my runaway thoughts and bring me back, if only for a moment, into Jesus' presence.

Although this is not possible in many workplaces, as a Christian organization we have tried to introduce a daily prayer rhythm at Care for the Family. A rota offers three 15-minute slots at the beginning, middle and end of the working day. People can sign up to meet in the prayer room at the centre of our building or jump online to pray for the needs of the organization, for colleagues, or for anything that is on our hearts. It can be hard, amid the pressures of meetings and deadlines, to carve out the time to do this, but the opportunity is there!

But finding time to pray during the working day doesn't have to be the preserve of Christian organisations. Even if we are the only Christian in our place of work, can we make time in the flow of the day, even if just for a moment, to pause to be still – perhaps linking it to a regular activity like turning on the computer, making a coffee, or before jumping on a call – to invite God's presence into the moment? For those who work from home, we may be able to build other simple rhythms of prayer into the crevices of the working day. Perhaps we can take advantage of Zoom to plan a weekly prayer time with someone else at home, and the creativity of 24-7 Prayer rooms and prayer spaces all offer the possibility of time in the Father's presence.

I have discovered that as we invite God into our day, he sometimes surprises us by breaking into the mundane, perhaps bringing someone across our path or speaking to us in new and unexpected ways. The story of my coming to work for Care for the Family began with a 'chance' meeting in a coffee queue, and my experience of seeking to 'divert daily' is that 'coincidences' like these increasingly become part of the warp and weft of life. While there have been times when God has been silent, there have also been many times when the gentle nudge of the Spirit has brought clarity or direction to my day.

Often one of the hardest things about writing a book is deciding on a title. A few years ago the book I had written to help parents navigate the digital age was at the publisher's – typeset, designed and ready to be printed – but still without a title. With hours to go before the publisher's deadline, I was flicking through the newspaper and turned the page to read the phrase 'left to their own devices'. Of course, that could have been a coincidence, but on that occasion I knew that in his kindness the Lord had given us a title. And the simple rhythm of 'diverting daily' means that we are more able to spot those nudges of the Spirit when they come.

WITHDRAW WEEKLY

The Bible tells us to rest every seven days. At various times in history people have tried to ignore this advice. After the French revolution, the government introduced a ten-day week. The idea was that people would work for nine days and then rest. But the new system failed. There is something about the seven-day cycle that is at the heart of creation.

Since I was a child, Sunday has always felt different to the other days of the week, but I generally saw it as an integrated part of 'the weekend'. When our children were little, the weekend would involve seeing friends, shopping, sport and catching up on jobs, and on Sundays we would add going to church, roast chicken and apple crumble into the mix. My children can recount many stories of being sent up ladders to clean the gutters or to hold logs while Richard attacked them (the logs that is!) with the chainsaw on Sunday afternoons. It was a number of years before we made the discovery that the seventh day was different from a day off. So for us now, when we get it right (and we don't always), we try to make Saturday the day for catching up on jobs, doing the weekly shop, mowing the grass and the million and one DIY jobs on Richard's to-do list. Sunday is our Sabbath day – a day that is different.

In the next chapter, we will look in more detail at the challenges and benefits of practising the Sabbath, but suffice it to say, keeping the seventh day as a day of rest in a way that works for you is one of the best rhythms of life that we can adopt. As author Walter Brueggemann says: 'People who keep Sabbath live all seven days differently.'[71]

71 Walter Brueggemann, *Sabbath As Resistance: Saying No to the Culture of Now* (Westminster John Knox Press, 2014), p43.

ABANDON ANNUALLY

Shortly after we began our 'date night' routine, Richard suggested we go away for a weekend together without the children. It sounded a lovely idea, but to his disappointment I said no. My response was partly because I thought we would be overburdening friends in asking them to help out with our tribe, and also because I thought we were letting our children down in some way by heading off without them. I couldn't have been more wrong! Fortunately, common sense prevailed, long-suffering friends went above and beyond, and we had what came to be an annual routine of a couple of nights away without our offspring, just the two of us. But we had to fight for the time. Even when we did get away, issues that had been buried would come to the surface that needed to be resolved. In the long run, however, having time away together reaped dividends. And the same can be true of finding some extended time – just the two of us – in our relationship with Jesus.

Some seasons of life, particularly if we are parenting little ones, caring for elderly parents, or bringing up children with complex needs, may make this almost impossible; and whatever our circumstances or responsibilities, careful planning and creativity will be required. Even in my current season, in order to prioritize extended time alone with Jesus over other (good) things, I have to fight the temptation to see it as self-indulgent or a 'nice extra'. There are all sorts of ways we can mark out some time to do this. I have a friend who books a room at a retreat centre to enable her to switch off for 24 hours; other ideas might be heading off to a Christian festival (with a children's programme!), spending a night away with like-minded friends, or venturing into the great outdoors.

Of course, 'getting away' isn't always easy or even a possibility. Carla, a single parent, reflected that this is really a challenge for her. She said:

'Mostly it's as much as I can do to get through the day, and the last thing I can think about is planning time away. It's hard enough to get someone to look after the boys if I have a doctor's appointment, let alone for a retreat. But not long ago some friends, who knew I was struggling, offered to have the boys overnight so I could have time to myself. I couldn't afford to go away, and even if I could, I couldn't face it, so I had a retreat at home. I decided to be like Mary – to ignore all the jobs and to simply spend time with Jesus. It was hard not to be distracted but I went on a couple of walks, listened to music, painted – and slept. I didn't hear God speak in an earth-shattering way, but just having time to be with him without everything else piling in was a gift. In a way that's hard to describe, when the boys came back I felt I had a new lease of life!'

Sally, who cares for her elderly father, discovered the possibility of going on an online retreat. She said:

'I couldn't leave Dad, but I found I could engage with this retreat online. Of course I'd have preferred something face to face, but it was better than nothing. I really benefitted from setting that time aside, and I'm going to make sure I do it regularly during this season of my life.'

Whether we are tentatively putting one foot on the first rung of the ladder, or already have the T-shirt and are well-practised in the discipline of rhythms of retreat, the chances are that none of us will find this easy. We can read books, listen to podcasts and dream about encountering God in new and exciting ways, but actually marking out the time in the diary and then doing it is hard.

In our Care for the Family parenting seminars, we often tell parents that they are the 'keepers of the atmosphere' in the home – the 'thermostat' that sets the temperature, not just the 'thermometer'. In a similar way, there are things we can do proactively to set the right atmosphere and create the right conditions for our minds, hearts and bodies to be open to the presence and power of God's Spirit.

How we do this, will be different for each one of us, but I have found that to have a fighting chance of spending at least a few minutes in the Father's presence, I need to create the right atmosphere for me. Conveniently, the conditions for this all begin with the letter 'C'. My space needs to be Calm, Comfortable, Concealed and Carefree.

CALM

The soundtrack of twenty-first-century living has caused us to be accustomed to a barrage of sound assaulting our senses, with silence hard to come by. In fact, to prepare astronauts for the absolute silence of outer space (the quietest place in the universe), NASA has to train them for the experience. This involves immersing them in a chamber that blocks out 99.9% of all sound. The sensation the astronauts have is so extreme that they report hearing noises they have never heard before – their pulse, the pumping of blood around their bodies, even the creaking of bones and tendons.

I don't think there will be too many of us signing up for immersion in the NASA capsule, but perhaps we can find the equivalent of that chamber – a place to escape from the white noise of our lives; to be silent – if only for a few moments; and to tune our ears to the sounds that are so easily drowned out, in particular the still, small voice of God.

The book of 1 Kings tells the story of the prophet Elijah. After his celebrity success on Mount Carmel, Elijah flees for his life and finds himself on Mount Horeb. The Lord tells him: 'Go out ... on the mountain in the presence of the LORD, for the LORD is about to pass by' (1 Kings 19:11). A powerful wind comes, followed by an earthquake and then a fire. And after the fire comes a gentle whisper (1 Kings 19:11–12). The Hebrew phrase for a gentle whisper means 'a voice of thin silence'. God wasn't in the wind, the earthquake or the fire. He made his presence known to Elijah out of the thin silence.

A number of years ago, I had the privilege of visiting St Paul's Cathedral in London, and one of the highlights included a tour of the remarkable Whispering Gallery, famous for its perfect acoustics. Thirty metres above the cathedral floor, a walkway circles inside the great dome. If you ignore the noise of the crowds below and lean in to the wall, whispered words can be heard as clear as a bell across 137 feet. And it is when we find a place of calm where we can lean in to the thin silence, that we may hear the gentle whisper of God.

I have to work hard to be comfortable with silence, and I often fight a losing battle with the wanderings and wonderings of my mind. When Jesus visited the home of Martha and Mary, we find Martha whizzing around preparing the meal, while Mary is ignoring all that there is to do, and simply sitting at Jesus' feet (Luke 10:38–42). Finding a place of calm may help my body slow down enough to be a Mary, but my whirring mind is often still like a Martha.

When discussing this with my friend Carol, she confessed that she had the same problem. Within seconds of starting to pray, her mind veers off in all directions, one thing leading to another, until minutes later she realizes what is happening. She said:

> 'I end up feeling so guilty and upset with myself, I've often just given up and decided that I'm too useless and unspiritual, and that God is thoroughly disgusted with me. But now when this happens, I tell myself not to cave in. I ask God to forgive my inattention and to help me concentrate, and I start to pray again. I've come to believe that he would rather I do that, than not pray at all.'

The mantra 'Pray as you can, not as you can't' has helped me in this. Try setting a timer just for a few minutes and gradually going from there. There is nothing you have to say, and nothing you need to prove. Just breathe, abide, and be still.

It is in the calm, quiet moments that I have glimpsed a little of what Mother Teresa meant when she gave her enigmatic response to questions by journalist Dan Rather in a now-famous interview. His first question was to enquire what she said during her prayers. She replied: 'I listen.' Dan then asked: 'Well then, what does God say?' Mother Teresa smiled and answered: 'He listens.'

Of course, not everyone will be in a season of life where longer periods of silence are even possible, but whatever our shift pattern, however early our children wake up, or however many emails beckon, can we set aside just a few minutes at the beginning of the day to be still? A few minutes with no agenda apart from spending time in the presence of the one who loves us? A few minutes in which we can allow him to set our compass for the day ahead.

COMFORTABLE

I need the space to be comfortable. A few years ago I was given an old Anglican prayer stool. I was so excited at the gift and thought it would be the silver bullet for a renewed prayer life. In kneeling on the exact spot where saints of old had prayed, I figured that surely some of the richness and depth of their glorious prayer lives would rub off on me. Suffice it to say, my enthusiasm was short-lived. Whoever the stool was designed for must have been considerably taller than me with knees of steel! It is made from a beautiful piece of oak, so while looking the part, it has to be the most uncomfortable piece of furniture known to man and does nothing to encourage me to enter the inner sanctuary of God's presence. Spending time with him is meant to be enjoyable, not a Spartan test of endurance. We need to find a place where we feel comfortable – though perhaps not so comfortable that we nod off! Like the lioness, we can be attentively still – alert to the present moment.

For me now, that place is a little leather armchair in my study. The chair is special to me; I bought it shortly after my father died with some money he left me and with the express purpose of setting it apart as a place to pray. It is a comfortable place where, with a good cup of coffee, I can be still for a few moments before the activity of the day begins.

CONCEALED

I need the space to be concealed. Although I long to share the joy of spending time in God's presence with my children, and especially grandchildren – 'to make visible the invisible' – I also need it to be a place that is hidden. Jesus said to his disciples: 'But when you pray, go into your room, close the door and pray to your Father, who is unseen' (Matthew 6:6). Phone off. Door closed. Time together. A picture of intimacy.

My job means that I am often on the road and there can be days on end when I am nowhere near the secret place of my little room and my leather chair. While the Premier Inn's purple armchairs are an adequate substitute, I have also discovered another secret place that I can go to any time of the day or night.

One of my favourite childhood books was *The Secret Garden* by Frances Hodgson Burnett. Its heroine is ten-year-old Mary Lennox who is sent to live with her uncle in a large English country house after her parents die of cholera in India. When a servant tells her about the walled rose garden in the grounds that her uncle locked up years ago after the death of his wife, Mary is helped by a little robin to find the key to the door. The secret garden is overgrown and uncared for, but Mary begins to tend it and over many months the garden becomes a place of life and redemption, not just for her but for others in the story. In my mind's eye, I can be in that beautiful walled garden in an instant. It is a secret place and only I have the key. And at any time and in any place, I can go to it to spend time with Jesus. As comfortable as they are, the formality and anonymity of hotel rooms when I'm on tour – particularly if I feel that something hasn't gone as well as I hoped – can occasionally lead to feelings of loneliness and isolation. So just as Richard and

I have to work hard at keeping in touch when I am away, I need to be intentional about making space to sit in this garden. And when I do, it becomes my refuge and hiding place, a place of relationship and restoration.

I am inspired by what author Johannes Hartl writes:

> The human spirit has the capacity to know God. To know God?! That is just unbelievable! The uncreated, eternal, limitless God? Yes, exactly! And because of this, the secret is so massive. And it gets even better! There is a place in you where you can meet this God … In the biblical story of Creation, God puts mankind in a garden …
>
> The term 'garden' was not understood in biblical times to be the kind of mixed landscape of broccoli beds, box hedges and children's swings that we know today. A garden was a luxurious park for rich people, an extremely beautiful place. And what happened there? Very simple: God and man met each other. In a way, our own hearts are like a garden for meeting with God.[72]

I loved hearing Tim Mackie from the Bible Project expand on this theme. He explained that the word 'paradise' in both Greek and Old Testament Hebrew means 'garden' and throughout Scripture this is one of the most potent symbols to convey the place where heaven and earth meet, a place of heavenly abundance exploding with life. And a place where we can experience God's perpetual presence.

CAREFREE

Finally, I need the space to be carefree – in particular, free of distractions. Distractions come in many forms. There are external interruptions – WhatsApp messages, Instagram feeds, children needing attention, people calling by, a pile of admin in my line of

---

72 Johannes Hartl, *Simply Pray* (Muddy Pearl, 2018), p18.

sight, as well as internal distractions – the worries and concerns that are so often the wallpaper of our lives.

If I am to create a carefree space, I've learnt that I must acknowledge that there are some distractions I *can't* do anything about. But there are things that I *can* do something about, and I need to take action to deal with them. This includes turning off notifications, putting my phone on silent and preferably out of sight, choosing to ignore beckoning tasks, welcoming random thoughts as a springboard to pray, or jotting them down to return to later.

When we have decided to set aside a period of time in which to be open to the presence of God – whether it is five minutes or an hour – it is good to make sure we really do have that amount of time. If we are keeping an eye on the clock because there's a cake in the oven, an elderly parent to take to an appointment, an office call waiting, or a football match to referee, this will only distract our focus. For some of us, there are just too many distractions at home or at work, and it will be easier to go for a walk, sit in the car or find a quiet bench to sit on outside – any place where we can be carefree and undisturbed. One mother told me her carefree space was the back step of her house. She said: 'I grab a cup of tea and just take five minutes when I can – it's a lifesaver!'

This is not rocket science, and there is no set formula to follow. We are simply creating space, inviting God to join us, and trusting him to turn up.

When he gave the Sermon on the Mount, Jesus tackled this issue head on: 'Give your entire attention to what God is doing right now, and don't get worked up about what may or may not happen tomorrow' (Matthew 6:34, MSG).

When we learn to make room for the interruptions of life, anchor ourselves in God's presence through our everyday activities and give our entire attention to what he is doing in the moment, we will find, as Dallas Willard famously said, that little by little 'our minds will return to God as the needle of a compass constantly returns to the north'.[73]

Time and again God makes his presence known in the ordinary things of every day. We just need to live in such a way that we have the capacity to notice.

Moses was doing what he always did – tending sheep in the desert of Midian – but something that day made him venture a little further. The Bible says that he came to Horeb, the mountain of God:

> There the angel of the LORD appeared to him in flames of fire from within a bush. Moses saw that though the bush was on fire it did not burn up. So Moses thought, 'I will go over and see this strange sight – why the bush does not burn up.'

EXODUS 3:2-3

And it is as Moses stops what he is doing and turns aside to look at the bush that God speaks. Just as the lioness from her place of attentive stillness scans the horizon, notices movement, and springs into action at the right time, can we order our lives so that we notice the movement of God on the horizon, see something we might otherwise have missed, and, like Moses, turn towards it?

This concept is beautifully captured by the poet Elizabeth Barrett Browning:

> Earth's crammed with heaven,
> And every common bush afire with God;
> But only he who sees, takes off his shoes,
> The rest sit round it and pluck blackberries.[74]

---

73 Dallas Willard, 'Personal Soul Care', in *The Pastor's Guide to Effective Ministry* (Beacon Hill Press, 2022), dwillard.org (accessed 13 March 2023).
74 Elizabeth Barrett Browning, 'Aurora Leigh', in Nicholson and Lee, eds., *The Oxford Book of Mystical Verse* (OUP, 1917).

PAUSE TO CONSIDER:

- *What would help you to create the best atmosphere in which to spend time in God's presence?*

- *Where and when in the past have you experienced God's presence in a tangible way?*

- *Where would you go in your imagination to spend time with Jesus?*

CHAPTER 13

HUNTING AND PROVIDING

> Giraffe provided [Elsa] with great fun too. One afternoon, when we were out with her, she took on fifty. Wriggling her body close to the ground and shivering with excitement, she stalked them, advancing step by step.[75]

We had recently said farewell to student days and the ivory towers of academia, and many of us already had taken the next step on life's journey. The church was putting on a workshop about living our faith on the 'frontline', and a number of us gathered in a dingy church basement, the familiar green china cups and saucers laid out ready for the coffee break. Notebooks at the ready, we were eager to glean wisdom for the road ahead. To our bemusement, the speaker began by holding up two pieces of fruit – an orange and a peach. 'What's the difference between these?' he asked. 'And what do they have to do with faith in the workplace?'

We gazed at the objects in question: both round, both orange-coloured, and both fruit. An awkward silence followed, as none of us had the slightest idea what he was talking about. It was only when the speaker took a bite out of the peach and then began to peel the orange, carefully separating each segment, that his point became clear. He was talking about the sacred/secular divide. 'We can easily treat our lives like an orange,' he explained. 'A segment for work, another for leisure, and yet another for spiritual formation. However, life should be like a peach. Our faith journey is integral to *the whole of life*.' Theologian Emil Brunner expands on this idea when commenting on our working lives: 'The Christian community

---

75 Joy Adamson, *Born Free* (Pantheon Books, 1960), p21.

has a specific task … to regain the lost sense of work as a divine calling.'[76]

Our work is as much a place where we can 'keep company' with Jesus, as he urged us to, and learn to be in a place of attentive stillness, as every other area of our lives.

On the first pages of Scripture, we are introduced to a creator God who is at work, and his work is 'very good' (Genesis 1:31). When God placed Adam and Eve in the garden, the plan wasn't for them to be on permanent holiday, relaxing in deckchairs on the bank of the Euphrates, sipping piña coladas in the cool of the day. We read in Genesis that 'The LORD God took the man and put him in the Garden of Eden to work it and take care of it' (Genesis 2:15). As children made in his image, the opportunity for us to have joyful, creative, and meaningful work is part of God's original plan.

Those who face long-term worklessness and unemployment can testify to the debilitating effect it can have on our wellbeing. It is an issue that was particularly highlighted during the Covid-19 pandemic when the UK government introduced the furlough system whereby people could be laid off their jobs during lockdown but were still paid. It was an incredible scheme that no doubt saved many businesses from going under. During the pandemic, I carried on working and simply swapped my office desk for the kitchen table. On some days, the litany of Zoom calls and the tyranny of Microsoft Teams meetings, with the need to pivot and find new ways in which our organization could meet the needs of families, meant that there were occasions when that piña colada beckoned, and furlough sounded an attractive option! So I was surprised to find that many of my furloughed friends begged to differ. They reported feeling lethargic and despondent, sensing that their lives lacked meaning and purpose.

Another unexpected consequence of Covid-19 was the recognition of the immense value of jobs that had previously been

76 Emil Brunner, *Christianity and Civilization* (Scribner's Sons, 1949), p69.

under the radar. On Thursday evenings during lockdown, people stood on doorsteps, at open windows, in gardens and on balconies, banging saucepans and sounding horns to show gratitude and appreciation to frontline health workers. But this was the tip of the iceberg. The incredible contribution made by cleaners, postal workers, hairdressers, delivery drivers and those in many other roles we had previously taken for granted was also brought into the spotlight.

No role is insignificant. Scripture reminds us: 'Whatever you do, work at it with all your heart, as working for the Lord, not for human masters' (Colossians 3:23).

The recent social media phenomenon of 'quiet quitting' is the polar opposite of working at something with all our heart. Originally a protest against a long-hours culture, quiet quitting means doing only what your job demands and nothing more. You still show up for work, but stay strictly within the boundaries of your job description, doing nothing extra. So no more helping out colleagues or staying late to finish a task.

While some jobs have clear boundaries on time, others may be more fluid – early starts, staying late, engaging in pastoral care or responding to emergencies go with the turf. But whatever our work, doing it with all our heart doesn't mean grinding ourselves into the ground. A friend worked in an office where long hours were the norm. He told me the culture was so toxic that colleagues tried to cheat the system by leaving an untidy desk and a jacket on the back of their chair after they had gone home to give the impression they were working late. It wasn't long after our conversation that he handed in his notice. A culture of performative busyness is the polar opposite of working 'with all your heart'. It might look productive, but if the aim is to impress demanding bosses by looking busy all the time, it can lead to an unhealthy, people-pleasing attitude and eventually to burnout.

Boundaries around work are essential, but not as an indelible line in the sand. Working 'with all our heart' means that we are willing to be flexible when needed – and sometimes to accept that we may be required to go above and beyond the call of duty. I am constantly impressed by the strength of character shown by a colleague at Care for the Family, in particular his willingness to go the extra mile. Granted, these tasks are part of his role, but if someone needs to open up the building early or stay late, sort out a car to go in for servicing or drive the breadth and length of the country to bring home a team member who has tested positive for Covid, Julian is your man.

Those who work part-time know that a degree of flexibility is required and my own current role is no exception. There have been some entertaining moments! Media opportunities rarely fit in a neat nine-to-five timeframe and, on one occasion, I had agreed to accept an opportunity to speak on BBC radio the following day, even though it was my day off. Out of sight, out of mind … at 10.30am the next morning I was relaxing in the hairdressers, coffee and magazine in hand, mid-highlights, when my phone rang. It was the BBC letting me know that the programme would be going live in four minutes. Momentary panic ensued until my long-suffering hairdresser downed tools and created a pop-up studio in the (thankfully empty) nail salon upstairs. Although my highlights stayed on longer than they should, mercifully no cameras were on. I was able by God's grace to pivot in the moment – and the listeners had no idea!

Our attitude to our work is more important than we realize. Interestingly, the same Hebrew word, *avodah*, is used for both work and worship, and in a very real way our work can be part of our worship to God. Whether we are tidying up toys after the toddler group, repairing a burst pipe, painting a mural, crunching numbers for the end of year accounts or preparing a sermon a job well done gives glory to God and the opportunity to pause and be thankful to him.

If life is a peach, not an orange, it follows that the workplace offers a wonderful opportunity for us to grow in our discipleship and discover more of the 'easy yoke' and freedom that Jesus offers.

Over the years, I have studied and been employed full-time, part-time, paid and unpaid. I've been a stay-at-home mother, had a boss, been a boss, worked in an office, worked from home and worked on tour. And in every one of those roles, I have experienced a tug-of war between the demands of work and home. A number of years ago when the clamour was at its loudest, a friend gave Richard and me some wise advice. He suggested there were five spheres where we could invest our energy: paid work, voluntary work (including church activities), and relationships with family, with friends, and with God. In order to regain a sense of peace and freedom, he advised us to rank these in order of their importance to us, and then to use that as a benchmark for decision-making about how we spend our time in the future.

It was great advice, and those priorities have since helped us decide what things to say 'yes' to and what things to lay down. And they still help us today.

Not everyone has the privilege of having a job they love, and I am grateful for a job that in so many ways fits my skill set, personality and temperament. But it hasn't always been like that. There have been many other roles over the years when I've had to work outside my gifting, when relationships have been strained, when I've felt bored and unfulfilled, when tasks have felt way outside my comfort zone, when things haven't gone according to plan, and when I've had to deliver difficult feedback. I don't expect many of us have verses from the book of Leviticus pinned to our fridge or to our Twitter feed for daily encouragement, but this ancient book reminds us that holiness isn't some fluffy, otherworldly quality; it is pursued in the gritty engagement of everyday life. Good relationships, fair weights and measures and wholesome speech are all mentioned – all of which may be forged in our lives through engagement in the workplace. And work isn't limited to paid employment – volunteers, carers and especially parents are included.

When I was a stay-at-home mother, I remember wrestling over what to put in the box on a form that asked me about my profession. How did I describe the role of wiping snotty noses, refereeing sibling disputes, tying shoelaces, untangling knotted hair … in fact, doing all that is involved in raising the next generation? The little box just wasn't big enough.

Many parents struggle with their identity, and guilt comes with the territory. They can feel guilty if they are at home, worrying that they are 'wasting' any training they may have invested in. If they head out to work, they can feel guilty for neglecting their family. And working from home or working part time can sometimes feel the worst of all worlds. I have had some spectacular misses. There was a time when our son broke his arm playing football and the school was unable to contact me on the phone, so a friend was summoned to take him to hospital. I only discovered the drama several hours later, after his arm had been set in plaster. Or another occasion (a moment of 'helicopter parenting'!) I was ferrying forgotten football boots to school, only to discover I had to answer to the wrath of a very disgruntled boss who had been expecting my presence at an important meeting.

One of my very first holiday jobs was as an office receptionist. As well as choosing cream cakes for the partners' weekly meeting, part of my role was to put all the post through the franking machine before the sacks were collected at the end of the day. In the first week, I will never forget the feeling of job satisfaction as I put the last letter through the machine with fifteen minutes to spare, followed quickly by the sickening realisation that I had made a big mistake. Instead of 10p and 12p (this was 1980!) I had set the machine wrongly and all the letters had gone through at £10.00 and £12.00 instead. I tied up the sack and prayed no one would notice, but seconds later my conscience prevailed. I will always remember the kindness of so many people that day. A clear direction never to make that mistake again, but wrapped around with grace. No recrimination, no judgment – just kindness and understanding.

All the secretaries had to stay late and re-address the envelopes (and there were many), and the offending ones were packaged up and sent off for a refund. That lesson stood me in good stead on other occasions when I have messed up – when I reversed my boss' car into a metal post in Yeovil magistrate's court car park, missed a deadline, forgot an appointment; lost my notes; and a million other things besides. But perhaps even more precious, it taught me to respond with clarity but also with grace when the boot was on the other foot and it was someone in my team who had messed up. When things haven't gone according to plan, we can be tempted to beat ourselves up with a litany of 'if onlys'. It is then that we need to lay down the voice of guilt in whatever guise it comes and hear the Father's voice reminding us that we have nothing to prove.

My personality means that I very much live in the present. Of course, like everyone, I make plans, but I am seldom future-focused and, unusually, any job I have ever had has been the result of a 'chance' meeting or invitation. There is nothing wrong (and a lot right) about a clear plan of action, as long as we remember the caveat from the book of Proverbs: 'We can make our plans, but the LORD determines our steps' (Proverbs 16:9, NLT). The Bible warns us against 'selfish ambition' (James 3:14), whereas godly ambition – ambition for the things of the kingdom – is commended.

Alongside the question of ambition is the nature of 'calling'. Not everyone has the privilege of working in an area that brings them fulfilment. Sometimes we have to do a job we don't enjoy just to put food on the table, and if that is the case, we can perhaps look to other areas in our lives to bring us fulfilment. But those who are able to work in an area that aligns with their personality, gifting and sense of purpose will find it is an 'easy yoke'.

The queen of fragrance, Jo Malone, began concocting her signature scents in her kitchen at an early age and she has often spoken about the joy and identity she finds in her work. In a 2021 interview with *Harper's Bazaar*, she spoke about the perfumer's 'ability to capture a moment'[77]:

> 'We're gatekeepers of scent memories,' she says. 'They take you to places and times; you can close your eyes, and you're right there in the moment ... the greatest creativity often comes from the smallest amount in your hands.'[78]

Jo Malone sees her inspiration and calling stemming from her belief in God. In her autobiography she explains:

> When it came to my beliefs, I didn't have any kind of lightning-bolt epiphany; it was something that developed gradually. The more you stand close to something, the more you sense its familiarity and that's what finding God felt like: a faint voice in the distance that grew louder until it became sure and clear.[79]

That sounds to me like the easy yoke.

Despite the joy and opportunity that work can give, the writer of Ecclesiastes shoots a warning across the bow:

> *My heart took delight in all my labour,*
> *and this was the reward for all my toil.*
> *Yet when I surveyed all that my hands had done*
> *and what I had toiled to achieve,*
> *everything was meaningless, a chasing after the wind.*

ECCLESIASTES 2:10-11

Creative, fulfilling work is good – just not too much of it. If we look for significance in our work, we will come away empty-handed. God

77 Roberta Schroeder, 'Jo Malone: "The best creativity comes when you have the smallest amount in your hands"', *Harper's Bazaar*, 4 March 2021 (accessed 25 February 2023).
78 Ibid.
79 Jo Malone, *My Story* (Simon & Schuster, 2016), p111.

created meaningful work as a blessing, not an idol. The key is in the *rhythm* of work and rest.

The lioness we saw on that evening game drive was a fierce hunter and a provider. That was her nature. We saw her lying still and attentive, totally focused on her prey, motionless in the grass, perfectly positioned and waiting for exactly the right moment for the chase.

Early the following day, our guide took us out in the jeep again. Dawn was painting a new light across the open plain as we drove past the place where the lioness had been the night before. The patch of grass where she had been waiting so patiently was still flattened, but there was no sign of her. And then, a few yards further on, we saw her again. Lying under a tree with her cubs, and with the remains of the kill. Her night's hard work had been successful – and now she could rest.

PAUSE TO CONSIDER:

- *What does working 'with all your heart' (Colossians 3:23) mean to you?*

- *In what ways can you worship in and through your work?*

- *In what order of priority would you place the different areas of life where you invest your energy?*

- *How could you adapt the ways you spend your time to reflect your priorities?*

CHAPTER 14

TAKING TIME TO REST

You may have seen lionesses lounging around as though half asleep. Sometimes they even flip on their backs as they rest in the golden sunlight – like solar panels storing up energy for later.[80]

The daily rhythms of work and rest are all around us. Professor Nicola Slee describes this beautifully:

> There is an essential pause at the heart of all creative work and endeavour: the silence which is integral to music, to poetry and liturgy; the wide margins around the page when we are reading or writing; all that is excised from the poem or the painting, what is left out in order for what there is to breathe.
>
> I used to think gaps in between work were empty space, wasted time or at most, concessions to the weakness of mind and body: all that counted for work was the conscious explicit attention to the task – and I'd feel guilty or secretly triumphant that I'd managed to escape the burden of work when I was away from my desk. I've come to see that the rests and pauses, the moments or hours when the mind is idling, the day-dreaming, the walk along the beach and the long hours of sleep are, in fact an essential part of the work.
>
> We are not machines who can go on mindlessly, hour after hour, day after day, but human beings with our mysterious rhythms of ebb and flow, receiving and giving, ingesting and outpouring. 'It is in vain,' the psalmist says, 'that you rise up early and go late to rest, eating the bread of anxious toil; for he gives to his beloved sleep' (Psalm 127:2, ESV).[81]

80 Lisa Bevere, *Lioness Arising: Wake Up and Change Your World* (Waterbrook Press, 2011), p153.
81 Nicola Slee, *Sabbath: The hidden heartbeat of our lives* (Darton, Longman & Todd Ltd, 2019), pp90–91.

At the beginning of the day Richard and I say a prayer that asks God to order our work *and* our rest. Pushing ourselves 24-7 may feel heroic, but if we run ourselves ragged with insufficient rest it not only impacts our overall well-being but our ability to be present with God.

Jesus himself modelled the importance of rhythms of work and rest. In the Gospels we read that he sends his disciples out to heal the sick and cast out demons. They return from the mission trip brimming over with stories to share. But Jesus appears to have other priorities: 'Come with me by yourselves to a quiet place and get some rest' (Mark 6:31).

The rhythm of both work and rest is fundamental to our well-being. Athletes know that balancing stress and recovery is the key to maximizing performance, and a business culture that encourages a good balance of work and rest reports not only increased job satisfaction but greater productivity. In his days at Microsoft, Bill Gates would famously take a couple of weeks a year as 'Think Weeks'. He would head off to a remote cabin with a fridge full of Diet Orange Crush soda for company to spend time reading and reflecting. And the regularity of those two weeks a year away from his operational responsibilities apparently paid dividends on his return.[82]

While not many of us will be able to escape to our own cabin in the woods, it is striking that taking time out to do what looks 'unproductive' – to think and daydream and create – had such a profound impact on the success of Gates' business. Creating enough margin to allow for this wider perspective is clearly a deeply beneficial practice.

When I am working on a project, I can easily get absorbed and not notice where the time has gone. I'll find that I've been tapping

---

82 Juliet Funt, *A Minute to Think: Reclaim Creativity, Conquer Busyness, and Do Your Best Work* (HarperBus, 2021), p63.

a keyboard or staring at a screen for hours on end without a break. An exception to this was during lockdown when the regulations allowed us all to escape the four walls of our houses and head out for some fresh air. The usually quiet grassy area at the end of our lane was rammed with people jogging, walking dogs or doing sit-ups. It wasn't possible for everyone, but there was something about the routine of getting out of the house, even if just to walk round the block, that was attractive; we could step out of the day's busyness and reorder our thoughts.

The delightful film *The Most Reluctant Convert* tells the story of the life of C.S. Lewis. Much of the narrative is taken from his actual diaries and while watching the film I found myself drawn to the insight it gives viewers into his daily schedule.

8am – Breakfast
9am – Read and write
1pm – Lunch
2pm – Walk (with the winsome comment that 'walking and talking are two pleasures that should take place independently.')

I imagine that the discipline of taking time out to walk alone each day was key to Lewis' creativity and well-being. His circumstances may be very different from ours – he clearly did not have young children in tow! – but we can nonetheless learn from his example. We can consider what things count as 'rest' for us, and plan to make time for those things in our lives. My daughter, a farmer and mother to two small children, told me that heading out across the fields on the quad bike while someone watches the children brings her rest and restoration. A friend finds rest in simply pottering around the house, trying to regain some semblance of order. And a dad told me that after a busy day at work he found cooking and even washing up restorative.

I am grateful that I am a good sleeper – I can generally sleep at any time and in any place (to Richard's frustration). I can count on the fingers of one hand the nights when I have been watching the clock in the early hours. Sleep is one aspect of rest, but it is not always something that we can control.

Researchers have found that increasingly we are working longer hours and short-changing ourselves when it comes to sleep. Glowing screens, Netflix on demand, the draw of social media and, not least, the pressure to emulate captains of industry by proudly wearing the badge of 'needing little sleep' are just some of the reasons why the average night's sleep has decreased from eight to six hours.

I was fascinated by an article I read about a bird called the white-crowned sparrow. Migrating hundreds of miles along the west coast of North America from Alaska to Mexico and back again, this ordinary little bird has a super power: it can stay awake for as long as two weeks during migration, flying all night and foraging for food all day without any need for rest. The US Defence Department has invested time and money into studying the brain activity of these birds to see if anything can be learned that will enable humans to go without sleep *and* function productively. Sleep-deprived shift workers, new parents and Red Bull-fuelled students would also, I imagine, be keen to discover the secret. But despite the investment of millions of dollars into this research, it remains a mystery.

Where possible, getting enough sleep allows our body and mind to recharge, keeps our emotions in check and gives us increased energy. Most of us are at our best – less irritable, kinder, gentler and more loving – when we have had enough sleep. Our need for sleep reinforces the fact that we have physical limitations. It is God alone who needs 'neither slumber nor sleep' (Psalm 121:4).

Within the rhythm of night and day is the rhythm of Sabbath rest. Resting on the seventh day is perhaps the most powerful expression of how we can live in sync with the rhythms that God himself built into our world, yet it is the discipline that many of us find hardest to keep.

Author Wayne Muller warns us about this: 'If we do not allow for a rhythm of rest in our overly busy lives, illness becomes our Sabbath – our pneumonia, our cancer, our heart attack, our accidents create Sabbath for us.'[83]

The theme of rest is a rich vein running through Scripture. At the very beginning of the creation narrative, we read that God made the heavens and the earth in six days and then 'on the seventh day he rested from all his work' (Genesis 2:2). Working for six days and resting on the seventh is built into the fabric of creation.

This rhythm is reflected in the commandment that God gave to Moses on Mount Sinai. The people were to 'Remember the Sabbath day by keeping it holy' (Exodus 20:8). He gave this as the reason: 'For in six days the LORD made the heavens and the earth, the sea and all that is in them, but he rested on the seventh day. Therefore the LORD blessed the Sabbath day and made it holy' (Exodus 20:11). They were to rest because God rested.

Even in the wilderness, the miraculous provision of daily manna accommodated the Sabbath. The people could gather manna for six days, but the seventh day was the exception. On the sixth day they could collect double rations to store up enough so that on the seventh day they could rest (Exodus 16:4–5). It was a lived-out example of the promise that if they obeyed the command to rest, God would continue to care for their needs.

Fast forward forty years. A new generation are standing on the edge of the Jordan before entering the Promised Land. These people have grown up in the wilderness; they know nothing of being slaves in Egypt, and in repeating the commandments to them, Moses takes the opportunity to remind them of their heritage. They are to 'observe' the Sabbath, to guard it, and to celebrate it. The reason given this time is not because God rested on the seventh day, but to remind them that 'you were slaves in Egypt and that the LORD your God brought you out of there with a mighty hand and an outstretched arm' (Deuteronomy 5:15).

---

83 Wayne Muller, *Sabbath: Finding Rest, Renewal, and Delight in our Busy Lives* (Bantam Books, 2000), p1.

The economic system of Egypt was built on the back of slavery and Pharaoh was a brutal tyrant. No matter how hard the Israelites worked, his insatiable appetite for production of bricks meant it was never enough. As Wayne Brueggemann writes in his book *Sabbath as Resistance*:

> ... the Sabbath commandment looks back to the emancipating God of the Exodus who delivered from the restless productivity of Pharaoh and who rests on the seventh day ... In our own contemporary context of the rat race of anxiety, the celebration of Sabbath is an act of both resistance and alternative. It is resistance because it is a visible insistence that our lives are not defined by the production and consumption of commodity goods ... The alternative on offer is the awareness and practice of the claim that we are situated on the receiving end of the gifts of God.[84]

The word Sabbath (*shabbat*) means to stop or to cease. At its heart is the message that a period of ceasing and resting is a key part of the rhythm of life. It is a day for stopping ordinary work and for delighting and worshipping. And it begins with the need to acknowledge our humanness, the fact that there are limits to our capacity, and that if we work for six days and then stop, we can trust God to look after the seventh.

A seventh day of rest gives us the opportunity to step off the treadmill of production, achievement and consumption. When I was growing up, few shops were open on a Sunday, but today in shopping malls up and down the country it is business as usual. Sunday is a day to buy and consume like any other.

But as well as the draw of the shopping mall, one of the biggest challenges to the Sabbath can lie a little closer to home. Ironically, church life can pile on the activity. Busy Sunday services,

---

84 Wayne Brueggemann, *Sabbath as Resistance: Saying No to the Culture of Now* (Westminster John Knox Press, 2014), p85.

volunteering, and afternoon meetings can add to the demands of the day and make it a far cry from stopping, delighting and worshipping.

How we spend our energy during the week will inform what we need to do to rest. While some may have work that is physically demanding, those who have office-based jobs may have a less physically active day. When I am working from home, a step counter would reveal that my physical activity is limited to trips from my desk to the kitchen and back again. If our work is mentally, emotionally, or spiritually draining, stopping and being inactive may be the last thing we need and engaging in some kind of enjoyable physical activity will be the thing that restores our tired brains and weary hearts. And if running 10K is not our preferred de-stressor, how about taking a break from screens to read a physical book, having a long bath, enjoying a hobby or going for a drink with a good friend? In fact, doing whatever it takes to bring us the restoration we need!

As a practising Jew, Jesus kept the Sabbath not with rigidity and legalism, but with freedom and life. The Pharisees started out observing this day with zeal, but to ensure they didn't put a foot wrong, they codified hundreds of extra laws and regulations about what was and what wasn't allowed on the Sabbath.

And so it is fascinating that in Matthew's Gospel, immediately after Jesus invites the crowd to find rest for their souls by coming to him rather than trying to obey the burdensome laws of the Pharisees, there are two controversies about the Sabbath.

In Matthew 12:1, we read that Jesus and his disciples were walking through a cornfield one Sabbath afternoon. The disciples were hungry, and defying the Pharisees' extra rules, they picked some ears of corn to eat. The Pharisees were outraged and challenged Jesus about this. His reply was an insight into the heart of God: 'The Sabbath was made for man,' he said, 'not man for the Sabbath. So the Son of Man is Lord even of the Sabbath' (Mark 2:27).

We then read that:

> *Going on from that place, he went into their synagogue, and a man with a shrivelled hand was there. Looking for a reason to bring charges against Jesus, [the Pharisees] asked him, 'Is it lawful to heal on the Sabbath?' He said to them, '... It is lawful to do good on the Sabbath.' Then he said to the man, 'Stretch out your hand.' So he stretched it out and it was completely restored, just as sound as the other.*

MATTHEW 12:9–13

As a direct result of this challenge to their authority, 'the Pharisees went out and plotted how they might kill Jesus' (Matthew 12:14).

The scandal Jesus caused wasn't just his challenging of their legalism, but because he was announcing the breaking in of the kingdom of God – the beautiful reign and rule of God that will be the ultimate rest.

Finding a Sabbath rhythm will be harder for some of us than others. Our personalities and temperament will come into play – it is not something that I find easy – and our circumstances, family responsibilities and work commitments may make 'stopping' a challenge. We may have children who have team fixtures on Sundays, and if we take Sunday as our day of rest, we will need to decide how we approach this. We may have elderly parents we need to care for, friends we want to invite over for a meal, involvement in kids' church or setting up and packing down after the services. On the farm, my daughter and son-in-law still need to feed the animals on a Sunday and other jobs will also make it difficult to put one day completely aside. However, the important thing is to start where we are at and discover habits that will work for us in our situation now that will help us stop, delight and worship. 'Sabbath as you can, not as you can't.'

Here are some principles about Sabbath that might be helpful:

A DAY TO TRUST

Just as the people of Israel had to trust God to provide for their needs, we need to trust that we can work for six days and rely on God for the seventh. If Sunday is our rest day are we able to trust that the work we have put into Monday's presentation is enough (even though we know that tweaking the PowerPoint and going over the script a few more times would make it better)? Can we trust that jumping off social media for 24 hours won't jeopardize our fundraising campaign?

A DAY TO REST

Ask yourself what rest looks like for you. We spend physical, emotional, social, mental and spiritual energy every day, so what is it that we can do on the seventh day to bring life and replenish us in these different areas? What things for us are 'work' and what are 'rest'? While I enjoy the results, gardening is effort for me, but I have a friend for whom pottering around her garden with a trowel brings her unbelievable joy and refreshment. I love having people over for Sunday lunch; that, for me, is (usually) rest and delight, but for others it can be hard work.

A DAY TO PREPARE FOR

'The day of preparation' in the Bible was the day before the Sabbath when all the preparations for the next day were made so that it could be enjoyed with others to the full. Putting in the work up front so that we can enjoy the Sabbath might mean making sure that we finish those emails, do the shopping, get ahead on the cooking or sort out our pile of admin. It's not always realistic to prepare and plan for everything beforehand (especially with young children!) but we can, at least, aim to do whatever is possible to enable a genuine day of rest.

A DAY TO RECEIVE AS A GIFT

Jesus said, 'The Sabbath was made for man' (Mark 2:27). So instead of Sabbath-keeping – adhering to a puritanical list of dos and don'ts – can we reframe our thinking and embrace it as a gift? Spending time being thankful for God's goodness and generosity is a great place to start. The Italians have a lovely concept called *dolce far niente* which means 'the sweetness of doing nothing'. Sit still, if only for a moment, and allow your thoughts to wander. As the saying goes: 'Time you enjoy wasting is not wasted time.'

A DAY WITH A BEGINNING AND AN END

In the creation story, God begins the day at sundown, and the first week begins in the evening. The Jewish Shabbat begins at sunset on Friday evening and ends after dark on Saturday, but there is no absolute rule as to when our day of rest should start and end. Those who work on a Sunday need to be creative and find a different time to have their Sabbath. And some find that a ritual of some kind – perhaps lighting a candle or saying a prayer – can be a great way to mark its beginning and its end.

A routine of resting on the seventh day can bring life and health to our lives. There is some irony in the fact that it takes effort to rest. But it is worth the effort. Christian scholar and philosopher Dallas Willard warned us: 'If you don't come away for a while, you will come apart after a while.'[85] Or as the saying goes: 'When you go against the grain of the universe, you get splinters!' If we can find a rhythm of rest that works for us, it will spill over into the rest of life.

Resting on the seventh day isn't about adding one more thing into an already full schedule; it is about making a paradigm shift to realign the way we live. If we can make our rest day the apex of our week, we will find it works its rhythm into the cadence of our lives, and we will become restful in a more permanent and constant way.

85 Dallas Willard, quoted in Ruth Haley Barton, *Invitation to Retreat: The Gift and Necessity of Time Away With God* (InterVarsity Press, 2018), p1.

PAUSE TO CONSIDER:

- *When do you 'down tools', try to stop the thoughts racing around your mind and rest? What makes it difficult for you to do this?*

- *Which of the principles about resting on the seventh day do you think you will find most helpful as you begin to 'Sabbath as you can, not as you can't'?*

CHAPTER 15

EMBRACING THE SEASON

> We found that Elsa marched well until about nine in the morning, then she began to feel the heat and kept stopping wherever a rock or bush gave shade. In the afternoon she was reluctant to move until five; after that once, her pads had hardened, she could have gone on all night.[86]

I was sitting on the beach with our grandson. We'd spent the last half hour building a magnificent sandcastle and were now watching the tide come in, waiting for it to do its inevitable work of demolition. The evening sun caught the white crest of the waves, and we sat mesmerized as one after the other they broke on the shore. Watching the rhythmic advance of the tide, my grandson questioned me in a manner worthy of a cross-examination at The Old Bailey: 'Granny, why are there waves? ... Why does the water come in? ... Why does it go away? ... Where does it go? ... When will it come back?' It seemed that each answer I gave him was then drilled down with a million further 'whys' until his three-year-old curiosity was satisfied.

An old expression says that 'time and tide wait for no man', and as we sat watching the tide coming in, turning and retreating, the gravitational forces of the moon orchestrating this dance time and again, I was reminded of the beautiful rhythm and order of creation reflected in this insightful account in G.K. Chesterton's book *Orthodoxy*:

> Because children have abounding vitality, because they are in spirit fierce and free, therefore they want things repeated and unchanged.

86 Joy Adamson, *Born Free* (Pantheon Books, 1960), p52.

They always say, 'Do it again'; and the grown-up person does it again until he is nearly dead. For grown-up people are not strong enough to exult in monotony. But perhaps God is strong enough to exult in monotony. It is possible that God says every morning 'Do it again' to the sun; and every evening, 'Do it again' to the moon.

It may not be automatic necessity that makes all daisies alike; it may be that God makes every daisy separately, but has never got tired of making them. It may be that He has the eternal appetite of infancy; for we have sinned and grown old, and our Father is younger than we. The repetition in Nature may not be a mere recurrence; it may be a theatrical *encore*.[87]

The writer of Ecclesiastes reminds us that 'there is a time for everything, and a season for every activity under the heavens' (Ecclesiastes 3:1). The cold frosts of winter giving way to the green buds of spring, long balmy days of summer followed by golden autumn colours, and then shorter days and longer nights ushering in the cold winter months once again. Marked by the wonderful variety of changes in weather and hours of daylight, each season brings its own opportunities and challenges and requires different ways of living – cranking up the heating or putting on those extra layers in the winter, or lighting the barbecue and gathering round the fire pit on a long summer's evening for (at least some of!) the British summer.

As well as the seasons of nature, there is a rhythm in the universe that orchestrates life itself. The rhythms of night and day, waking and sleeping, working and resting, eating and drinking, breathing, and the beating of our hearts. We thrive within the steady beat of the rhythms of life.

We experience different seasons in the workplace, in health, in friendships and in family life. Twenty-somethings will generally have the energy and opportunity for spontaneity that slips away

87 G.K. Chesterton, *Orthodoxy*, Christian Heritage Series (Canon Press, 2020), p61.

from us as life's responsibilities take over. New parents are likely to be physically exhausted, juggling the demands of small children while enduring acute sleep deprivation. I'm sure that many in this phase of life will have cheered inwardly (or even outwardly!) when the famous tidying guru Marie Kondo admitted that she had 'kind of given up' on tidying her own home after having had her third child: 'My home is messy, but the way I am spending my time is the right way for me at this time at this stage of my life,' she told *The Washington Post*.[88]

For parents, physical exhaustion may give way to the emotional rollercoaster of the teenage years, the empty nest and the 'too tidy' house. Retirement then requires us to change step again, and for those who become grandparents there is a new set of joys and challenges.

If discipleship is about the whole of life, it's important for us to give voice to the physical, emotional, social, mental and, in particular, spiritual needs and opportunities that we have in different seasons.

When I was a child, my family worshipped at an Anglican church where the altar cloth and vestments were a visual reminder of the different seasons of the church's year. I can still remember the sombre feeling of purple in Lent that was then replaced by a joyful burst of gold and white on Easter Day, and the same was true for the seasons of Advent and Christmas. Each season also had traditions that brought a rhythm and structure to worship.

Running alongside this are the individual seasons of our spiritual lives. We may experience a 'winter of discontent' when life is hard and God seems silent, a springtime of hope with new shoots of possibility, a summer of opportunity and blessing, or an autumn of change and letting go. And each season requires a different response.

---

88 Jura Koncius, 'Marie Kondo's life is messier now – and she's fine with it' *The Washington Post* 26 January 2023, washingtonpost.com (accessed 13 March 2023).

I remember that the habits that had served me so well as a twenty-something needed to change when I got married. And then, with the arrival of children, they were blown out of the water completely. The daily dawn chorus of four little ones meant that my pre-children 7am quiet time was impossible. It took a while for me to accept this, to stop feeling guilty and to discover new patterns that suited this season. Sometimes a snatched prayer during a night time feed at 3am was the most my tired body would allow. And parenting in the teenage years saw the need to readjust yet again. While there were some days when my old routines were more achievable, I discovered there was still opportunity to pray at 3am – this time as I lay awake waiting to hear the key in the door.

To fast forward a few years, our children have now left home and I've been in a season of life which, although I've been enjoying to the full, has also been a stretch physically, emotionally and spiritually. In addition to leadership in the workplace and in church life, and keeping our home in some semblance of order, I've had welcome opportunities for writing and speaking in the UK and abroad. And alongside a delightful brood of grandchildren to provide childcare for has been the responsibility of caring for elderly parents. I am someone with a reasonably big capacity (my underlying propensity for ant-like behaviour is never far away), but even so, this has been a challenge. I knew that I was keeping afloat – but only just; and going forward, I didn't want the people who were most important to me, and in particular, my relationship with Jesus, to be relegated to the margins.

I had been invited to a tea party to mark a friend's retirement, and to my delight I found myself sitting by someone whose work and home life in many ways mirrored my own. Keen to mine the depths of her wisdom, I expressed my desire to reduce my commitments, but confessed that I had no idea where to start. I'm not sure if I thought she would offer me a silver bullet (I tend to think that if there was one, I'd have discovered it by now), but the question she asked that afternoon over the cucumber sandwiches brought about a paradigm shift in my thinking: 'What, for you,' she asked, 'is the gift of this season? What has God given you to steward during *this* stage of your life?'

Finding the answer didn't happen instantly, but it did prompt me to step back and reflect – to identify the season I was in, and, in particular, ask what my unique responsibilities were at this time. What were the distinctives of my life now compared to my younger self 'x' years ago? What were the opportunities and challenges? What were the things that only I could do? And perhaps more importantly, what were the things that I could lay down because they belonged to a different season?

Seeing the season as a gift that God was asking me to steward well gave me a new lens to look through. In addition to making decisions to free up time for family responsibilities (in particular, childcare for my grandchildren), I was able to recognize that tasks I was finding wearisome and demanding were, in fact, an opportunity for God to continue his never-ending work of shaping my character more into his image.

Reflecting on the different seasons, I realize that I have often fallen into the trap of thinking that a slower day is coming, convincing myself that when the children are at school/work is less pressured/church life has quietened down/the children leave home … *then* I will have more time to be spiritual. But perhaps one of the greatest insights I have received is the realization that a slower day isn't coming. We need to make time to enjoy God's presence *now*, right in the midst of the unique challenges and opportunities that each season of life brings.

Part of my work at Care for the Family involves delivering the content for online resources to strengthen family life. We have a brilliant team whose skills involve creating sets, lighting, filming, sound recording, editing and content management. It's a privilege to work with such a gifted set of people and the recording days nearly always now run smoothly, but it hasn't always been like that! The travel restrictions brought about by Covid-19 meant that, like many organizations, we had to quickly pivot and discover new ways of working. For us that meant adjusting to deliver our events online. And the learning curve was steep.

Early in lockdown we gathered to record one of our first online parenting events. Phones were off, the clapperboard clapped, cameras started to roll, and over the following minutes we recorded the first section. We cut – and it was then that it happened: it seemed that everyone on the set started to chip in with their ha'penny worth of advice on how we could improve things. 'It would be better if you moved to the left … sat down … stood up … swapped that paragraph round … used a different word … changed that quote … wore a different coloured shirt … rolled up your sleeves …' and so on. Every comment came from a good heart and the desire to make this the best resource possible for families, but there were just too many of them, and by the end of the morning my head was spinning.

A few more frazzled recording days followed until one of the team called us all together. He reminded us that while in the days leading up to the recording everyone's contribution was valued and welcome, on filming days we had to be mindful of our individual roles. We each had a gift to bring and a part to play, and we needed to stick to it. That reminder for the team on filming days to 'stay in your lane' has become part of our DNA as an organisation. And the same principle is true in our discipleship. Our task as followers of Jesus is to know our role during the particular season of our life that God has gifted to us – to discover the contribution that only we can bring and to stay in our lane. And as we do that, we will experience more of the 'easy yoke' that Jesus offers.

PAUSE TO CONSIDER:

- *How would you describe the season you are in at the moment? What is its gift to you?*

- *Is there anything from a previous season in your life that you can now lay down?*

- *What is the particular gift you have to offer in this season of your life?*

CHAPTER 16

BELONGING TO A PRIDE

When I arrived alone [Elsa] gave me a great welcome but it was heartbreaking to see her searching everywhere for her sisters. For many days to come she gazed into the bush and called for them. She followed us everywhere, evidently fearing we might too desert her.[89]

I am challenged by Dietrich Bonhoeffer's words: 'Let him who cannot be alone beware of community … Let him who is not in community beware of being alone.'[90]

I recently had the wonderful opportunity to record some family podcasts in the US. At the end of the trip, the available flights home meant that I had a free day in Colorado Springs. I decided that I would explore some of the incredible mountain trails in the area, however, when I told my hosts, it became evident that they were not so keen on this plan. They said that if I set off solo there was a chance that I wouldn't be on my own for long! I could be joined by a mountain lion or a bear. Lion and bear attacks usually happen when people are by themselves and my friends decided that it would not only be safer but much more fun if they joined me. As well as showing me the way, their presence would ward off bears or other predators. 'It's better together' they said.

This is not just true in the mountains of Colorado.

Richard and I have eaten pasta with Silas and Annie on alternate Tuesdays since our children were small, meeting to chat about the joys and challenges of being young parents, of marriage, and of ministry. The evening nearly always follows the same pattern:

89 Joy Adamson, *Born Free* (Pantheon Books, 1960), p14.
90 Dietrich Bonhoeffer, *Life Together* (SCM Press, 2015), pp57–58.

food, wine, good conversation, lots of laughter, occasional tears, and praying together. We have forged a deep friendship which has stood the test of time. We have given one another permission to speak into each other's lives. If Richard and I are showing signs of being niggly or irritable with each other, Silas or Annie will usually challenge us as to whether we are spending enough time together, and similarly, we try to hold them to account. We have sought guidance together on big decisions, stood by each other in crises, and celebrated the joys of life together.

While meeting together has been a delight, it has also required intentionality and discipline to keep going. There was one period of time when Richard and I had allowed other commitments to get in the way of our Tuesday night suppers. We missed one and then another, and before we knew it a couple of months had gone by. It was Silas who called it. I still remember his words. 'Guys, are we still serious about this? If we are, we need to agree dates and stick to them, but if not, we may as well not bother.'

Faithful are the wounds of a friend. Of course, sometimes things get in the way – I may be on the road, or we may have visitors or family commitments – but where possible, we make an effort to prioritize those evenings together. And that relationship has become precious to us. The Bible says that 'iron sharpens iron' (Proverbs 27:17) and in that respect, Tuesday nights have been a blacksmith's forge for the four of us.

One of Richard's life verses is from Hebrews:

> *And let us consider how we may spur one another on toward love and good deeds, not giving up meeting together, as some are in the habit of doing, but encouraging one another – and all the more as you see the Day approaching.*

HEBREWS 10:24–25

While much of this book has focused on finding space for the presence of God individually in our lives, we don't do that in a vacuum.

The digital age means we are more connected than any other generation yet, at the same time, many are more lonely and isolated than ever before. In a culture that encourages fierce independence, we need community and relationship. It was what we were made for. Rugged individualism and doing life on our own are not part of God's design for humans to flourish.

God is relational. Father, Son and Holy Spirit live in a triune community of love together, and their relationship is at the heart of the universe – a thread that runs throughout Scripture. In the creation story, God shares his nature with us, creating both Adam and Eve. As we have seen, they are to care for the garden together, but also to create families and live together.

Throughout the Bible, God works through family and relationships. He promises the people of Israel: 'I will walk among you and be your God, and you will be my people' (Leviticus 26:12). And during his time on Earth, Jesus prioritized friendships and modelled living in relationship with others. As well as the band of twelve, Jesus had an inner circle of friends – Peter, James and John. These three were present during some of the more intimate times in his ministry, including when Jesus raised a little girl from the dead and at his transfiguration. And Jesus based himself at his friends' homes – at Peter's house in Capernaum when he was in Galilee, and with Martha, Mary and Lazarus when he stayed in Bethany.

Writing to the early church, Paul uses the analogy of the body to take up the theme of our interconnectedness:

> … *just as each of us has one body with many members, and these members do not all have the same function, so in Christ we, though many, form one body, and each member belongs to all the others.*

ROMANS 12:4–5

If we are seeking to grow in spiritual formation, we can't do it alone; we need the support and encouragement of others. We need a community to practise with, to knock off our rough edges, and to shape our lives. In the early days of Methodism, John Wesley and his followers would gather together in small groups. No doubt they discussed the more mundane things of life, but top of the list was the penetrating question: 'How is it with your soul?' And having asked each other the question, they would wait for the reply.

In my desk drawer at home there is a stash of well-thumbed notebooks of all shapes and sizes, scribbled in from cover to cover. These books are precious to me as they represent years of reminders of things to pray about, for two of my closest friends. We began meeting together when our children were small. We would drink coffee, eat cake and chat about life, and then one of us would look after the children while the others had an oasis of time to pray. The following week, a different one of us would draw the straw that represented childcare – and so it went on. The detail of how our relationship works has been different in the different seasons we've been through, but over the years we have prayed each other through the tapestry of life – morning sickness, sleepless nights, first days at school, broken legs and broken hearts, challenges in the workplace, conflict in the church, financial worries, and caring for elderly parents. Throughout all this we have sought to remember to ask what was possibly the most important question of the hour, 'How is your soul?', and to pray accordingly.

As we strive to grow in spiritual maturity, we can recognize that we hold in tension our individual commitment to grow in our discipleship to Jesus, while at the same time acknowledging that we can only fully live this way in community in interdependent relationship with others.

Members of the Order of the Mustard Seed community are encouraged to find a *cymbrogi*. *Cymbrogi* is an ancient Celtic term meaning 'companions of the heart', and the idea is that we find a trusted Christian friend who will check in on us, challenge us and cheer us on. If we were part of a traditional monastery, we would be living in proximity with others who were on the same journey, our lives would be more transparent, and it would be hard to find a place to hide. Depending on our own circumstances, we may have to work a little harder to achieve something of that sense of community, and key to this are committed friends who 'see' us, warts and all, and to whom we give permission to speak into our lives and to encourage us.

We have been part of a home group that meets together regularly, and an important part of those evenings has been eating together. Although the food doesn't need to rival *MasterChef*, inevitably it has taken more time, effort and preparation than boiling the kettle for tea, but it has been worth it. Something about sitting round the table together has given the opportunity for deeper conversations that might not have taken place in the more formal setting of a Bible study.

In some challenging times of life, we have been so grateful to this little group who have often gone the extra mile to support us. Over and above the difference their prayers have made has been the impact of the tangible love and care we have received, and that we will never forget.

Ben reflected on the importance of caring friends during a difficult time at work. His team weren't meeting their targets, relationships were strained, jobs were on the line, and he felt responsible:

'The game changer was when I was finally honest to my prayer group about what was going on and how it was affecting me. They stepped up and gave me incredible support. One evening after work some of them came to the office to worship and to pray into the situation. Another time a friend prayer-walked round the building while a difficult meeting was going on inside. Just knowing they were there for me made such a difference.'

Lin has been part of a home group in her church for many years. She commented:

> 'There have been some ups and downs and the occasional falling out, but over time we have built an incredible trust and friendship. People share what is going on in their lives, but they don't have to explain everything as everyone already knows the context and what the challenges will be. I feel known and loved. There is nothing else like it.'

Relationships in community work both ways. Rocks in a river change the direction and flow of the stream, but the stream, in turn, also moulds and shapes the rocks. And in the same way, just as our communities shape us, we also shape the communities we belong to.

Of course, at one level, we can only be responsible for making choices that shape our own spiritual formation, but at another level we can also make decisions and model practices that nurture our life together in community. The DNA of a community is not established by accident. How we treat each other, how vulnerable we are, our priorities and values can all be shaped by the example we set.

As a leadership team at Care for the Family, we have tried to build strong relationships that we hope spill over into the whole organization. Of course, at different times we are either more or less successful at this, but with family at the heart of our charity's mission, it would be ironic if we didn't try to prioritize our relationships. One way we do this is to have a regular 48 hours away together. It can be a challenge with so many conflicting diaries, but these occasions have become one of the most important parts of our lives. They are not deep-dive, off-site business development huddles, but something quite different. As well as working hard, we also make sure we have plenty of time to reflect, pray, eat, laugh and play hotly contested games of *Articulate* together! Rather than stoking the frenetic pace of leadership, it is an oasis, where we can be present to God and also to each other. Looking back, the seeds for some of the most significant decisions we have made have been sown during these times away, usually with someone tentatively beginning: 'I've been thinking ...'

But before we get too dewy-eyed about the power of relationships in community, it is worth reminding ourselves that the rubber often hits the road closer to home. In the fourth century, John Chrysostom, one of the early church fathers, famously called the home 'the little church'.[91] It is in the home that the foundations of discipleship are laid, a place where we can learn to get along together, to manage disagreement, to argue well, to forgive and be forgiven, to love and be loved. Building strong relationships within the family are part and parcel of our discipleship, requiring effort and intentionality. And undergirding all our relationships is the need to make time for each other.

In Chapter 6, we looked at how we can be pacesetters in our family life. Over the years, Richard and I have discovered that this applies not just to our children's activities, but to our own. When I am on the road speaking about family issues in different cities and locations around the UK, I usually head off on a Tuesday and return at the end of the week. Weekends of irritability and missed expectations have taught Richard and me not to stack the diary on my return, but to leave space to reconnect. We both love seeing friends, but very occasionally prioritizing time together can mean declining a fun invitation – simply for the reason that we know we need to spend time together.

The place where we hope to find like-minded followers of Jesus with whom we can build relationships with is ultimately, of course, the local church. In the turbulence of our post-Covid times, it is vital that we find an anchor point in a community of faith. A place where we feel secure, comfortable, able to be ourselves. A place where we can give and receive a home.

91 John Chrysostom, quoted in Daniel Grothe, *The Power of Place: Choosing Stability in a Rootless Age* (Nelson Books, 2022), p148.

Richard and I belonged to the same church for forty-five years, and our cluttered attic and overflowing garage bears witness to the fact that we have lived in the same house for thirty-five! Over the years, when we looked at others whose lives appeared to be much more exciting and adventurous, we have been tempted to feel that we were a little boring. So I was intrigued to come across the Benedictine vow of stability. Staying put in the same place is, it seems, neither dull or boring. In fact, because it gives us such a strong anchor to our community, it could be one of the most important ways we have of being able to nurture deep relationships. One of John Stott's tips for effective evangelism was apparently: 'Don't move house!' In a culture that prizes isolation and transience, it's easy to fall into the trap of commodifying our relationships – 'serial dating', window shopping for the best option, moving location and swapping friendships for ones that look more colourful and exciting. As Daniel Grothe says in his excellent book *The Power of Place*: 'God doesn't judge the fruitfulness of our lives based on the *quantity* of people we are around but by the *quality* of our service to the people around us.'[92]

We all have different circumstances, and some of us are called to keep moving, but for Richard and me, staying in the same city, in the same home and having the opportunity to build deeper, accountable friendships has been very precious and not something we take for granted. Staying put gives what experts call 'social capital' – the wealth of a network of mutually supportive relationships.

And there are lessons in this from the plain. In contrast to the solitary cheetah, panther or leopard, lionesses are the only members of the cat family to live socially in prides. They live in mutually supportive communities – hunting, feeding and resting together, not only caring for weaker lionesses but also looking after each other's young. And in the wonderful design of creation, the

92 Ibid, p23.

reproductive cycle of the lionesses synchronize so that cubs are conceived and born at the same time, which gives them a much better chance of survival and ensures the future of the pride.

Which brings us back in a full circle. In the Bible, when God chooses Israel, he speaks of them collectively – 'For you are a people holy to the LORD your God. The LORD your God has chosen you out of all the peoples on the face of the earth' (Deuteronomy 7:6). The language used in the New Testament to describe God's people is communal. And the point about transformed lives is that they lead to transformed communities that are greater than the sum of their parts. Community isn't just a means to an end, but the pinnacle of God's plan to form a people for himself.

PAUSE TO CONSIDER:

- *Do you find it more of a challenge to be alone or to be in community?*

- *Who do you have in your life that you can share your soul with? Who are your* cymbrogi *– your companions of the heart?*

CHAPTER 17

BORN FREE

Suddenly she stopped sniffing the wind and, with her head stretched
out, went off at a fast trot, leaving us behind. A few moments later,
in the far distance, we heard the faint call of a lion … George called
to her. She walked away from us. When George repeated his call
she only trotted faster along the game path until we saw the black
tuft on the end of her tail switch for the last time through the bush.
We looked at each other. Had she found her destiny? She must have
heard us; by following the lions she had decided her future.[93]

I had read the book *Born Free* as a child, but it was fascinating to
discover it again as an adult. The narrative tells the story of Elsa the
lioness through excerpts from Joy Adamson's diaries. I have no idea
what the Adamsons believed and their book isn't about faith, but
as I held this old hardback with its ripped dustcover in my hand, I
was intrigued to read the subtitle: 'A lioness of two worlds.' Those
words reminded me of our calling as followers of Jesus – he whose
kingdom is not of this world and who calls us to live in this world,
but not of it.

Then turning to the first page, my heart skipped a beat as I read the
quotation there. It was some verses from the Bible – Acts 22:27–28.

Paul is in prison and the Roman officer in charge has discovered
that he is a Roman citizen. The officer is curious and asks Paul how
that could be possible. He says, 'I had to pay a large sum of money
for my freedom.'

There is a momentary pause, and then Paul looks the officer
in the eye. 'Yes,' he replies, 'but I was *born free*' (verse 28, my
paraphrase).

93 Joy Adamson, *Born Free* (Pantheon Books, 1960), pp114, 123.

And, of course, we, too, are born free. Not as citizens of Rome, but as citizens of the Kingdom of Heaven. Jesus paid the price for us to have that incredible privilege. It is as we keep company with Jesus and walk with the Spirit in our everyday lives that we step into that freedom. Jesus says:

> *I'll show you how to take a real rest. Walk with me and work with me – watch how I do it. Learn the unforced rhythms of grace. Keep company with me and you'll learn to live freely and lightly.*

MATTHEW 11:28-30 (MSG)

The productivity of the little ant is admirable, but I am determined not to spend my life busily scurrying around in an effort to justify my existence. I want to be like the lioness. Not to have her grace and strength – as wonderful as that would be – but to live freely and lightly, from a place of attentive stillness. Jesus offers us that place of freedom, a place where our burdens are light, a place of connection and intimacy with the Father, a place where we have nothing to prove.

I don't want this to be a vain hope, a pipedream. I am thankful for the lessons I have recounted in this book and hope that you will journey with me in putting them into practice.

Joy Adamson describes Elsa as a 'lioness of two worlds.' As she and her husband released her into the wild, they had no idea which world she would choose to make her final home. Although Elsa continued to visit the camp, Joy writes: 'by following the lions she had decided her future.'[94]

And like Elsa, I have decided my future: to follow the call of the lion of Judah, whose kingdom is not of this world; to daily take up the yoke that Jesus offers, which is easy and light; and in the busyness of life to live from a place of attentive stillness. And as I do that, I want to experience the Father's love in increasing measure, and to allow him to shape my identity, my calling and my purpose.

94 Ibid, p123.

As I look back over my journey I am reminded of the words of 1 Samuel 7:12 – a verse I shared with Care for the Family's staff on a significant day in our history. When Care for the Family began in 1988, we worked out of an office the size of a broom cupboard – a far cry from the organization it is today. God's provision for us over the years has been incredible, and in January 2019 we were able to move into a new building, complete with a recording studio and auditorium. We had no idea what was coming down the road. Just a year later, Covid-19 stopped us being able to speak to families face to face. But we had the new facility. In God's perfect timing we were able to produce online material to support families through lockdown and beyond.

On the day we moved into the new building, all the staff gathered in an act of worship to remind each other of God's hand on our journey so far. During our time together I read a passage from the book of Samuel. The people of Israel were at war with the Philistines and the Lord had just won a great victory. To remember this, Samuel set up a stone and 'named it Ebenezer, saying, "Thus far the LORD has helped us"' (1 Samuel 7:12). We wrote that verse on the blackboard in the office kitchen as a daily reminder, not only of how far we have come, but that it has been the Lord who has made it all possible.

And in the same way, as I look back at my journey of learning to be still and to be attentive to the presence of God in my life, I know that thus far the Lord has helped *me*. It is only by his grace that any change has been possible.

From the outside, perhaps it might seem that not very much has changed – there is more margin in my day, but my life is still full. However, I know that on the inside, over the years, *everything* has changed. There has been a paradigm shift in how I experience the presence of God.

If left unchecked, my personality will default to performance, so I am grateful for the understanding that, as important as it is to have good spiritual habits and practices, transformation is ultimately the work of the Spirit in our lives.

I used to think that the demands of everyday life were an obstacle to spiritual formation. That one day, when life slowed down, I would magically become contemplative, experience God's love in greater measure, and be more interruptible, more kind and more loving as a result. But I now see things a little differently. The very things I thought got in the way of spiritual formation are, in fact, a means of grace, and the doorway to transformation. And it is as I lay down the striving and find time to be attentive to the love of God in me and around me, that I see with new eyes that his presence is available every moment of every day, underpinning the whole of life.

I know there will be ups and downs along the way. The busyness will creep back in, distractions will beckon, priorities will get skewed, and challenges will come my way; but when I fail, like Paul, I can remind myself: I have been *born free*.

My prayer is that the Spirit will take our efforts and that not only will we experience freedom in the way we live, but little by little, with increased discernment and clarity of vision and purpose, the effect will ripple out and bring transformation to our families, our communities and beyond.

> Lucy buried her head in his mane to hide from his face. But there must have been magic in his mane. She could feel lion-strength going into her. Quite suddenly she sat up.
>
> 'I'm sorry, Aslan,' she said. 'I'm ready now.'
>
> 'Now you are a lioness,' said Aslan. 'And now all Narnia will be renewed.'[95]

95 C.S. Lewis, *Prince Caspian* (Geoffrey Bles, 1951), p127.

Muddy
Pearl